The Sign of the Burger

In the series
Labor in Crisis
edited by Stanley Aronowitz

The
Sign
of the
Burger

McDonald's and the
Culture of Power

Joe L. Kincheloe

Temple University Press
PHILADELPHIA

Temple University Press, Philadelphia 19122
Copyright © 2002 by Temple University
All rights reserved
Published 2002
Printed in the United States of America

⊗ The paper used in this publication meets the requirements of the
American National Standard for Information Sciences—Permanence
of Paper for Printed Library Materials, ANSI Z39.48-1984.

Library of Congress Cataloging-in-Publication Data

Kincheloe, Joe L.
    The sign of the burger : McDonald's and the culture of power /
Joe L. Kincheloe.
        p. cm. — (Labor in crisis)
    Includes bibliographical references and index.
    ISBN 1-56639-931-9 (cloth : alk. paper) — ISBN 1-56639-932-7
(pbk. : alk. paper)
        1. McDonald's Corporation.   2. Fast food restaurants—Social
aspects.   3. Restaurant management.   4. Consumer behavior.
5. United States—Social conditions—1945–   I. Title.   II. Series.

TX945.5. M33 K57 2002
338.7'6164795—dc21

                                                    2001041447

To those who have worked hard to expose McDonald's culture of power:
Jose Bové
Tristan Kading
Dave Morris
Helen Steel
The Founders of McSpotlight

Also dedicated to the B.F.G.

Contents

Introduction

On the morning of August 12, 1999, Jose Bové and a band of fellow French sheep farmers descended on a McDonald's restaurant under construction outside the village of Millau. Angry that the 851st McDonald's in France was being constructed in their backyard, Bové, his accomplices, and a group of several hundred supporters parked their tractors, forklifts, and Citroens on the restaurant lot. With chainsaws, chisels, hammers, and screwdrivers, the group literally dismantled the half-built structure and carried it away piece by piece. In a media-driven, globalized world, the group's actions were perfect for television coverage.

The images that appeared on news programs around the world included the tractors and forklifts carrying pieces of the restaurant to the lawn of the regional magistrate's office in Millau, farmwives passing out Roquefort cheese to villagers to protest against McDonald's power to undermine local food production, and Bové himself toting a huge McDonald's sign. "Good visuals," as the media people say. Those arrested for their actions came to be known as the "McDonald's Ten" and quickly gained popularity throughout France and all over the world (Williams, 2001); Bové himself received such acclaim in Europe that some observers employed the term "Bovémania" to describe the phenomenon ("Think Global," 2000).

Bové elicited this response by using McDonald's sign value, its symbolic capital, to connect the profound European concern with food to the expanding worldwide fear of

1

the excessive power of transnational corporations. The paragon of a transnational company with huge assets and political-economic power, McDonald's saw its kinetic energy appropriated by Bové and redeployed in the construction of his own media image. Very sophisticated in his awareness of signifiers, symbols, and "the sign of the burger," Bové understood that McDonald's conveys diverse meanings to different individuals. In an interview in June 2001, he observed that people around the world see McDonald's very differently than many Americans do. In many places outside the United States it is viewed as a symbol of affluence and wealth—inside the United States it is not (Jeffress, 2001).

Taking the stand at his trial, Bové continued his analysis of the meanings of the McDonald's signifier: "McDonald's is the symbol of standardization of food," he said, adding an American simile: "What we did was like the Boston Tea Party" (Williams, 2001). Continuing this semiotic theme, the symbolic dimension of McDonald's vis-à-vis Bové—and McDonald's in general—attracts scores of interpreters. Journalist Tom Wheeler (2001), describing Bové as a "farmer for our time," asserts that his attack on McDonald's makes him the most compelling symbol of "the worldwide counterattack of peasants and family farmers against corporate agriculture . . . and global trading blocs organized by the big capitalist powers." Other observers identify McDonald's as the most important signifier around the world for free market capitalism and Bové as a leading symbol of opposition to it (Jeffress, 2001; Williams, 2001). And still other analysts refer to Bové as an enemy of modernist scientific progress (Watson, 1997b). These competing signs of the burger constitute a central dimension of this book.

McDonald's elicits responses like this in the United States and around the world. Americans are frequently baffled by the negative feelings many people outside the United States hold about their country. After the tragic attacks on the World Trade Center and the Pentagon on September 11, 2001, news programs portrayed shocked Americans asking why would anyone want to harm the United States. As one woman put it, speaking on CNN in the aftermath of the attacks:

> America has done nothing but help the world, often at great sacrifice to our own people. When people around the world have needed help, we have given it to them. Many have sacrificed their lives for people around the world. We have never done anything to hurt them. Why do they not understand that?

In this context Jose Bové's actions against McDonald's help us understand aspects of this anti-American sentiment. He disassembled the Millau McDonald's to protest against U.S. imperialism, trade policies, and the promotion of *malbouffe*, bad food (Williams, 2001). To many Europeans, Asians, Africans, and Latin Americans, McDonald's stands as a primary symbol for the Americanization of the planet, with all the environmental, political, moral, cultural, and economic dimensions of that process. When it comes to McDonald's and its relationship to America, we recall the Five Man Electric Band in the late 1960s exclaiming: "Signs, signs, everywhere a sign." McDonald's and America are signs for much of what is wrong with the contemporary world, Bové says:

> First, McDonald's represents globalization, multinationals, and the power of the market. Then it stands for industrially produced food bad for traditional farmers and bad for your health. And lastly, it's a symbol for America. It comes from the place where they not only promote globalization and industrially produced food but also unfairly penalize our peasants. ("Think Global," 2000)

McDonald's executives understand the widespread perception of their corporation as a signifier of America. One executive told me under the promise of anonymity (September 12, 2001) that after the terrorist-controlled airplanes crashed into the World Trade Center towers and the Pentagon, all McDonald's regional offices were closed and evacuated. A memo emailed to each office stated that the perpetrators were obviously attacking America directly, and since McDonald's represented America, company offices were highly vulnerable. In this case the executives thought the sign of the burger was powerful enough to get them and their staff members killed.

Thus, the symbolic meaning of McDonald's has taken on an emotional power similar to that of a flag or a ring. Bové's attack on McDonald's allowed him to appropriate some of the negative underside of this highly charged semiotic power, so that he:

- was hailed as a national hero in France.
- was compared to Robin Hood (Williams, 2001).
- was described as the new Vercingetorix—the revered warrior who led the Gauls against the Romans in 52 B.C. (Wheeler, 2001).
- was supported at his trial by 45,000 anti-McDonald's and anti-American demonstrators (Noble, 2000).
- received the adulation of thousands at an antiglobalization forum in Porto Alegre, Brazil ("Expelled French Activist," 2001).
- was cheered by residents of the West Bank town of el-Khader (Khalili, 2001).
- marched into Mexico City alongside Subcommandante Marcos and the Zapatistas (Williams, 2001).
- spoke in front of a McDonald's during the demonstrations against the World Trade Organization in Seattle as

protestors broke the restaurant's windows. (Seidman, 1999)

For another aspect of the signifying power of the Golden Arches, consider McDonald's role in the changes that have taken place in American education and the expansion of corporate power in everyday life over the past few years. In this market-driven neo-liberal era, many schools in the United States have accepted corporate intrusions into the classroom, and it is not uncommon to see corporate advertising and programming in American schools (Hoffman, 2001). Taking advantage of this new ideological climate, McDonald's has produced advertisement-laden curricula for almost every academic subject, including language courses in Russian, Spanish, French, and German (McDonald's Customer Relations Center, 1994).

Channel One (a for-profit company that offers free televisions to schools if they agree to broadcast its loosely defined "news programming" and, most important, numerous commercials) opened the gates, permitting McDonald's and thousands of other companies to occupy schools in the early 1990s. Students are required to view corporate television programming and live presentations (Boyles, 1998). The lesson corporations are attempting to teach students involves a form of scholarly passivity and acceptance of the data provided about political-economic matters (Boyles, 1998; Hoffman, 2001; Kincheloe, 1999).

Exemplifying this new corporate order, McDonald's was invited on May 22, 2001, to Stonington High School in Connecticut to provide career guidance during a required assembly. Among the students who walked into the school auditorium not knowing that McDonald's was involved was Tristan Kading, a 15-year-old sophomore. His story illustrates both the dramatic changes that have occurred in American schooling and the political atmosphere of the twenty-first-century corporatized cosmos. After a presentation on the advantages of working at McDonald's, the company's representative called for volunteers to participate in a mock interview. The first student selected made a masturbatory reference and was asked to return to his seat. At this point new volunteers were called for, and Kading was chosen. Ignoring the promptings of the McDonald's representative, Tristan used the forum to denounce McDonald's corporate policies—including practices leading to environmental destruction, lies about the use of beef tallow in preparing its French fries, and harmful farming methods (Raptorial Hall of Fame, 2001). Admonishing Kading that his comments would not get him a job at McDonald's, the representative ordered him to give back the microphone (Green, 2001).

School administrators immediately removed Kading from the assembly, describing him to the group as an "embarrassment to the school" (Green, 2001). The principal then demanded that the young man apologize to McDonald's in writing and read a second apology to students and teachers over the school intercom (Raptorial, 2001). In the broadcast apology, Kading described himself as a "bad student" whom no teacher would want to have in class (Green, 2001). In an interview with me after the fall 2001 term had begun, Kading confided that he should never have apologized for his comments. "Don't do anything," he said, "until you know your rights" (interview, September 20, 2001).

The message that the administrators and McDonald's sent to students is clear, Kading said: It is not acceptable to express your political opinions in school (Green, 2001). By early June Kading decided to leave Stonington High and the system that had consistently supported the administration's actions against him. After looking for another school, however, he decided to return to Stonington in September because he could not find one that was any better. Now, Kading reports, administrators avoid him and "try not to look at [him]" when he walks by. Unrepentant for his actions, Kading told me that he wants Americans to know that

> if this world is to have any extended future, McDonald's needs to be cut out. When you eat a hamburger, you're also eating a section of the South American rainforest and the air it purified. McDonald's is currently in a cozy situation as it seems our country is being run by a plutocrat, but hopefully we will see the problems McDonald's is creating even without the government shadowing our view before we have to start worrying about the world running out of oxygen. (Interview, September 20, 2001)

Kading's and Bové's relationships to the sign of the burger and its culture of power serve as fitting introductions to this book. Readers can sense in these episodes that powerful concepts and symbols are circulating around the Golden Arches—concepts and symbols that none of us (myself included) sensed in our first contacts with the corporation. In this circulation lie the conceptual origins of *The Sign of the Burger: McDonald's and the Culture of Power*. In this context the generative question emerges: Why is McDonald's a lightning rod for debate and discussion, an object of fascination, evoking strong feelings and emotions in the United States and around the world? Such a query leads us to the larger question: Why study McDonald's?

McDonald's serves as a widely recognized example that concretizes a plethora of larger social, cultural, economic, political, and educational concepts. The popularity of George Ritzer's *The McDonaldization of Society* (1993, rev. ed. 1996) has encouraged further analysis on these levels. The McLibel Trial in Great Britain, which pitted McDonald's battery of lawyers against two unemployed Greenpeace activists in the late 1990s, also raised public consciousness of the company's social, cultural, political, economic, and environmental role (Vidal, 1997). And, of course, McDonald's saturation advertising and founder Ray Kroc's Horatio Alger story of the "little company that made good" have contributed to its high public profile.

Analysis of such a well-known corporation allows adherents of different political and cultural perspectives to make ideological points about an institution with which people are intimately familiar. McDonald's "sign value" signifies far more than hamburgers. Indeed, the nature of the signification differs dramatically depending on whom one asks, illustrating the deep divisions both inside and outside the United States in readings of contemporary civilization. As I interviewed McDonald's employees and consumers from around the world, these dramatic differences revealed themselves in many different languages and accents. Such ubiquity and conflicting perceptions make McDonald's a symbol for an age.

The power of McDonald's to elicit dreams and fantasies from people around the world illustrates its compelling impact on the collective psyche. Numerous children I interviewed talked about wishing for an infinite supply of McDonald's hamburgers. Some wished they could someday own a McDonald's restaurant; many others wanted to raise hamburger trees on a fantasy farm they would someday run. One creative fanzine writer illustrates the importance of McDonald's in his consciousness and its power to infiltrate our fantasies:

> If Hollywood were to make a movie about a rogue McDonald's manager charged with turning a cadre of slip-shod but loveable ne'er-do-wells into a crack outfit of burger servin' prodigies in what Rex Reed would hail as "The Film of the Decade!"

then such a movie would be set here at this B-List McDonald's. Of course, this presupposes that Hollywood would make such a movie, which, after Hamburger: The Movie, they most decidedly will not. I mean, I wouldn't go to any feel-good movie about fast food restaurants and the callow employees there who learn an important life's lesson. Unless, of course, there was nudity. ("Philip," 1996)

Thus, McDonald's has captured the public imagination, playing many roles in the contemporary globalized society: all-American success story, creator of Happy Meal fandom, symbol of Western economic development, concrete representation of modernity, corporate bully, postmodern sign value, object of disdain, patron or cultural dislocator of McWorkers. I focus on the some of the more compelling roles in Chapter 1 and continue this effort in the following chapters, analyzing the nature of McDonald's sociocultural, political, and economic power. I concentrate particularly on the ways this culture of power has influenced—or, as I phrase it throughout the book, educated—America and the world. McDonald's educative or "cultural pedagogical" aspect involves its capacity to produce and transmit knowledge, shape values, influence identity, and construct consciousness.

The analysis of the Golden Arches' power dynamic, the power and domination McDonald's has constructed in the cultural realm, and the complex, never totally successful, ways it operates are the core concerns of this book. Vandana Shiva (1997) contends that McDonald's power has much in common with the pre-perestroika Soviet Union. The biggest difference, she argues, involves the ways the world has reacted to the two power wielders. Whereas the whole world was outraged by the concentrated, centralized control of the communist regime, most people are untroubled by the authoritarianism of transnational corporations that have no accountability to anyone.

Indeed, McDonald's the power wielder stands ready to do battle with anyone who messes with its power, with the positive valences of its sign value. The company understands the hegemonic worth of its signifiers as mechanisms of social regulation. George Ritzer sees McDonald's production process as an old-fashioned, modernist form of rationalization—an accurate understanding, for the most part—but the company's relationship to sign values is a good example of how the hegemonic process works in a postmodern context. Thus, the discourse about McDonald's generated by Ritzer and his supporters and critics, as well as this book (I hope), has an important relationship to some of the key debates of the early twenty-first century.

In this context we can see that McDonald's represents a new kind of business power—not a manufacturer or some other traditional form of industry, but an entertainment-based, fun-producing firm that extends to every last corner of the globe. Along with Coke and Disney, McDonald's produces power via pleasure. Significantly, this power-related (political) process takes place in the realm of culture—the sphere of society traditionally viewed as separate from the political. In the new electronic social order, the cultural realm becomes the most important venue of political socialization. This is a key theme of this book.

Another facet of "Why study McDonald's?" leads us to examine the website "McSpotlight" as a prototype for grassroots global democratic action in the twenty-first century. The unanticipated sociopolitical aspects of the McSpotlight debate room discussed in Chapter 1 do not diminish the important achievement of the website's founders. In the first three years of its existence, McSpotlight was visited 65 million times, making it one of the most important monitors of corporate behavior on the planet. Friends of democracy have much to learn from its organizers.

In this globalized context McDonald's operates in a landscape shaped by diverse logics and organizing motifs. This context suggests yet another response to "Why study McDonald's?" The Golden Arches exist in and respond to various sociocultural, political, and economic formations simultaneously and with little sense of the contradictions involved. For example, McDonald's operates on both a Fordist and a post-Fordist economic plane in the context of premodernist, modernist, and postmodernist cultural logics; it functions as a highly rationalized and as a transrational/affective organization, depending on the goal.

Given such multidimensional complexity, Doug Kellner (1998) asserts that a multiperspective analysis is needed. Taking his cue, *The Sign of the Burger* employs a mutually informative, synergistic bricolage of research methods, including ethnography, content analysis, historiography, cultural studies analysis, rhetorical analysis, semiotics, and critical hermeneutics. McDonald's is such a complex phenomenon that, as Kellner puts it: "The more perspectives one can bring to its analysis and critique, the better grasp of the phenomenon one will have and the better one will be at developing alternative readings and oppositional practices" (1998, p. xii). It is my hope that this book will not only help readers understand the Golden Arches in new ways but extend our thinking about research and interpretive processes as well.

A few brief definitions may be in order at this point to help readers unfamiliar with some of the contemporary jargon of cultural analysis and sociology. The terms "modernism" and "modernist" are used here to denote ways of thinking and modes of social organization that emerged as part of the scientific revolution beginning in Western Europe in the mid-seventeenth century. Understanding the failure of medieval ways of seeing the world, modernist thinkers sought new methods to understand and control the outside environment. Cartesian-Newtonian science became a foundation for this new impulse as it set out to make sense of complex phenomena by reducing them to their constituent parts for detailed analysis. Connected to modernism's scientific dimension is a socioeconomic one: capitalism, with its unyielding faith in the benefits of science and its handmaiden, technology, its doctrine of progress, its cult of reason and rationalism, and its logic of economic organization, which would culminate in the early twentieth century in Fordism.

The term "postmodernism" is used in complex and often confusing ways to designate both a philosophical position and a social era. Philosophically, postmodernism has something to do with the questioning of previously delineated modernist tenets. More specifically, postmodernist observers subject to analysis those social assumptions previously shielded by the modernist ethos. They admit previously inadmissible evidence, derived from new questions asked by once excluded voices, challenge hierarchical structures of knowledge and power that promote "experts" above "the masses," and seek new ways of knowing that transcend scientifically verified facts and "reasonable" linear arguments deployed in a quest for certainty.

"Postmodernist" is often used as well to describe the social condition of the globalizing electronic contemporary world. In postmodernity the grand narratives, the stories we tell to make sense of the world, are no longer believable; they fail to understand their own construction by social and historical forces. Reason is undermined because of its cooptation by those in power, who speak with the authority of a science not subjected to self-analysis. There is no way to simplify this definition of the postmodern condition. It is not a discrete, homogeneous historical period. All cultural expression in the contemporary era is not postmodern. In the economic domain, for example, post-Fordist flexible accumulation and emphasis on niche markets coexist with mass production of standardized products.

The postmodern condition is marked by a social vertigo that emerges from what has been referred to as "hyperreality" (Aronowitz and Giroux, 1991; Gergen, 1991; Smart, 1992). In this hyperreality individuals tend to lose touch with traditional notions of time, community, self, and history. New structures of cultural space and time, generated by electronic images bombarding us from local, national, and international sites, shake our personal sense of place. Electronic transmissions move us in and out of different geographical and cultural locales instantaneously, juxtaposing nonlinear signifiers and images of the world with downhome, folksy, and comfortable personalities who reassure us in the midst of the chaos. In this context many people are rendered vulnerable to the sign. Relinquishing the desire for self-direction in the thick semiotic jungle of hyperreality, they have difficulty making sense of the world and their role in it. Contact with such social and cultural dynamics makes it harder to generate commitment to anything (Kincheloe, 1995).

The Sign of the Burger is part of an ongoing conversation about McDonald's that includes the work of George Ritzer (1993, rev. ed. 1996) and John Watson (1997). Ritzer's *McDonaldization of Society* focuses on the ways in which the modernist hyperrationality of McDonald's organizational strategies elevates efficiency and standardization over questions of human needs and quality. The organizational plan forged by its founder, Ray Kroc, and the company's subsequent development fit well with the hyperrational historical trajectory of modernism. Ritzer's portrait of McDonald's is less important than his concern with the process of McDonaldization. We can learn much about hyperrationality, commodification, and dehumanization from Ritzer's analysis, but his reluctance to view McDonald's from diverse social locations—vantage points that provide us with a deeper sense of the McDonald's phenomenon and the complex ways it interfaces with and shapes the lives of people around the world—undermines the cogency of the analysis.

Golden Arches East: McDonald's in East Asia, edited by John Watson, attempts to address the shortcomings of Ritzer's approach by studying the role of McDonald's in five East Asian countries. Anthropologist Watson and his contributors explore the different ways in which these countries engage the Golden Arches, as evidenced by the specificities of consumer practices and the meanings individuals ascribe to their consumption. In this process the researchers are always concerned with testing the validity of Ritzer's McDonaldization thesis, especially as it concerns issues of standardization and cultural homogenization. Unless they are aware of this backdrop, many readers will not understand the authors' need to prove McDonald's lack of impact on local eating habits and cultural practices. Hence the central message of Watson's book: The corporation has blended so well into local East Asian cultures that it is no longer an American cultural icon or a wielder of power.

In these authors' analysis of East Asian consumption, McDonald's has little to do with larger sociopolitical and economic concerns. Indeed, Watson and his contributors, according to reviewer Samuel Collins (1998), do little more than affirm consumer behavior studies published in the *Journal of Consumer Research* and the *Journal of Marketing*. They consistently fail to grasp that contemporary advertisers intend for consumers to make their own meanings of products—it is an effective marketing ploy. This is why McDonald's customizes its foods for particular locations while concurrently clinging to the signifier of modern, advanced Americana—a semiotic tightrope. Thus, Watson et al. dismiss the power dynamics that I find so central to the story of the Golden Arches, arguing that the uniqueness of individual consumption erases concerns with the negative effects of globalization, transnational capital, and political-economic domination.

Such an analysis would dismiss Tristan Kading's concerns with environmental destruction and health, or McSpotlight's interest in the exploitation of children and low pay for workers, as not germane to the McStory. Consideration of problems like these would require researchers to move beyond asking narrow questions about specific meanings of consumption and raise social, cultural, political, and economic issues with interviewees. Observing the complex dynamics that emerge when the micro-social intersects with macro-concerns could have awakened the authors to another cosmos of meaning. In researching cultural-political artifacts, it is important not only to study consumption and production processes, but also to analyze how, say, hamburgers become implicated in diverse dimensions of culture.

This, of course, is what I am attempting to do in *The Sign of the Burger*. I begin in Chapter 1 by detailing the role of McDonald's in my own early life in the mountains of East Tennessee. In this context I document its role as a signifier of modernity and as such an escape route from my rural status. I tell my own story to help answer the questions "Why McDonald's?" and "Why study McDonald's?" Throughout the rest of the book I explore the ways in which individuals around the world have made use of the signifier of modernity, as I did. I provide examples of how much McDonald's matters to people in contemporary society, how much energy they are willing to expend—both positive and negative—in reference to its meanings. In Chapter 2 I analyze these meanings in an ideological context. Ideology is the process of protecting unequal power relations, and in this framework I study the many ways in which McDonald's produces ideology, as well as the ways in which different people receive it.

In Chapter 3 I focus on the postmodern aspects of McDonald's and the cultural dynamics that operate to extend its culture of power. Using the electronic power of communications media, a company can deploy signifiers under the radar of consciousness to shape attitudes and colonize desire in ways beneficial to its political-economic interests. In a society such as the United States where political literacy is in decline, such signifiers can exert a powerful subliminal effect. In Chapter 4 I extend my analysis of the company's political impact through the notion of McDonald's as public educator. McDonald's has played a significant role in the corporate reeducation of the American public to adopt a political-economic perspective that is more market-friendly, more accepting of unfettered free enterprise. I explore the ways in which this effort has been received by particular individuals, documenting examples of those who accept the reeducation project and those who reject it.

Chapter 5 probes the complexity of this educational role, analyzing the hegemonic aspect of the corporation. Hegemony is the process of maintaining domination in contemporary democratic societies by winning the consent of individuals to dominant forces of power. McDonald's wins this consent by attaching its signifiers to prevailing belief structures such as family values, patriotism, and nostalgia for a culturally homogeneous small-town America. In other countries around the world, McDonald's uses profoundly different if not conflicting signs to produce hegemonic power. With these understandings in mind, I explore McDonald's struggles to protect the sanctity of its signifying practices—the sign of the burger.

In Chapter 6 I detail McDonald's contemporary struggle to control the sign of the burger in the face of a variety of challenges. Since sign values in hyperreality are fickle, the corporation must keep up with day-to-day changes in the reception of particular signifying practices in an information-saturated world. Having endured a string of end-of-century marketing failures—the Arch Deluxe in 1996, Campaign 55 in 1997, and Beanie Babies in 1998—McDonald's in the first decade of the twenty-first century faces a historical watershed. When one adds the public relations disaster of the McLibel Trial, observers begin to understand the trouble in the Hamburger Patch. Confused by the mixed reception of its signifiers, the corporation is struggling to formulate new ways of representing itself in a rapidly changing world.

It is important in this context to describe my research methods. I began my research in the late 1980s and continued to collect data until September 2001. I approach interview-based research as a form of improvisational ethnography. In my experience, predesigned questions and formal questionnaires often assume a knowledge of where the interview is supposed to go and tend to shape the information obtained. With this in mind, I sought out individuals in naturalistic settings who often initiated conversations about McDonald's on their own volition. Sometimes, of course, I opened the conversation; at other times I encouraged interviewees to elaborate on their initial comments. As much as possible I engaged the inform-ant in a conversational tone and avoided the question-and-answer format of a formal interview. Because many of the conversations were spontaneous, I rarely used a tape recorder. I took notes on interactions that occurred:

- in McDonald's lines (queues) of customers waiting to place their orders
- with parents reflecting on their children's attitudes toward McDonald's
- with children describing their McDonald's experiences
- with audience members after my speeches on McDonalds
- with teachers and students in school settings
- with individuals in foreign countries speaking with me—the American visitor.

Many potential interviewees became uncomfortable when I followed up their comments with politically inscribed ques-tions, and they declined to offer further information. As I describe in the chapters that follow, some became angry with me when I asked or induced them in some way to react to political aspects of the McDonald's phenomenon. I consistently use pseudonyms to protect interviewees, though sometimes, when the information is relevant, I refer to their race, gender, and nationality. The notes on the inter-views are handwritten and stored in my personal files. In addition, I use information obtained from Internet websites and chatrooms. One problem that confronts researchers in the twenty-first century is that websites can quickly go from universally accessible to completely inaccessible, making it impossible to validate or challenge particular sources. As this book goes to the typesetter, all websites cited in the bibliography are available on-line. For those interested in pursuing some of the themes discussed in this book, the McSpotlight website offers an ever-changing and ever-expanding body of information.

In conclusion I would like to thank Stanley Aronowitz and Doug Kellner for their assistance in the publication of this book.

1 Why McDonald's?

I am driving my family from Miami to the mountains of East Tennessee to see my mother. It is 1993 and we are faced with hours of driving on the American interstate with its endless exits leading to the fast food fiefdoms. The kids are hungry and we stop at McDonald's. The restaurant is as familiar to them as a remote control. They know everything about it: how to deport themselves, how to stand in line, how to order, how to eat, and how to dispose of their garbage. So well do they know the menu that they have all decided what they will order before we enter. It is second nature to them. I, however, a first-generation refugee from the mountains, had to learn all of these cultural behaviors. There was a time in my childhood when there was no McDonald's. A significant change has taken place in just one generation in the United States—a change now migrating around the world.

Introduction: McDonald's and Being Modern

Beyond issues related to the public imagination, the American Dream, and the success of Western economic development, the questions "Why McDonald's?" and "Why study McDonald's?" hold personal meanings for me. McDonald's symbolized the modern, up-to-date "with-it-ness"—this was its appeal to me as a boy growing up in the rural mountains of East Tennessee. McDonald's helped shape my evolving identity and eventual entrance into the modern, if not post-

20

modern, America of the middle and late 1960s. To understand McDonald's, for me and millions of individuals around
the world, was to move from the backwoods to the cultural
center. For those of us from the hinterland, eating at
McDonald's was a cultural pedagogy in the ways and man-
ners of modernity.

I didn't want to remain a hick from the mountains. As I
later named my desire: I longed to be modern. As a hillbilly
I wasn't sure of the hip ways of dressing, acting, thinking, or
representing myself. In my cultural naiveté I saw McDonald's as a place where modern cultural capital could somehow be dispensed. I kept these memories in mind years
later, in the 1990s, as I monitored scores of conversations
about the Golden Arches and soon recognized that McDonald's is still considered a marker of a modern identity.

McDonald's ability to connect its corporate image to the
modern, to "what's happening?" is an important dimension to
keep in mind as we attempt to answer the question of why
McDonald's deserves such study. Vandana Shiva taps right
into this modernist dimension and its effect on consumer consciousness when she considers McDonald's invasion of India.
"There is," she told an interviewer, "a small middle class and
a tiny elite section that I believe feels inferior about what they
are, that has been so subjected to the pressures of Westerniza-
tion that they feel like second-rate Westerners, and people
would go in [McDonald's] for the experience not because of
what the experience is, but what it symbolizes" (1997).

As with modernity in general, McDonald's makes an East
Indian or a rural Southerner feel that he or she is getting
something better than anything experienced before.
McDonald's way of life involves something that is superior
to your food, your culture, your family, and your perceptions of the way you presently conduct your daily affairs.

Beans and Burgers

While I treasure many features of my Tennessee mountain boyhood, in no way am I romanticizing that place, that time. Most of my contemporaries and their families struggled to get by in the late 1950s and early 1960s. Few had money and few had hopes of a future much different from what they knew. Most held vicious racial and ethnic prejudices, and many of my male peers did not hesitate to cruelly exploit the women around them. It was always open season on queers, and the tortures reserved for those so designated were testimony to the sordid imagination of human beings. At the same time, there existed a collection of amazingly sensitive, creative, caring, and wise people who struggled with the pathology and violence surrounding them.

Members of this latter group, my parents were born in the mountains in the first decade of the twentieth century. Conceived 17 years after they married, I was granted a connection to a rural southern past via their stories of grandparents, parents, uncles, aunts, cousins, and other members of their extended families. My parents, unusually progressive in matters of race, class, and gender, provided me with the foundations of a critical consciousness that I would struggle to cultivate and extend throughout my life. They were strict teetotalers who used good food to replace liquor as a source of corporal pleasure. In a childhood with little purchased entertainment, I used some of my unstructured free time to watch my mother cook her ethnic cuisine: beans of every variety flavored with pork (fatback and ham hocks), fried chicken with a milk gravy, and cornbread baked in a black iron skillet. The aesthetics of her cooking were indelibly imprinted on my consciousness—so much so that the first time I studied a Jackson Pollock painting, I wanted to change his colors to browns, golds, and various shades of yellow to extend its resemblance to my mother's cornbread.

My mother's cooking, like that of so many rural southern women of her generation, was a subtle art form. She was the maestro of the bean—pinto, brown, October, great northern, navy, kidney, string, lima, butter, not to mention such beanlike legumes as black-eyed peas, field peas, and chickpeas. Her seven-bean salad was a favorite at church dinners and covered-dish suppers. After we moved from the country into a small Tennessee city, one of my friends observed that the Kincheloes never ate a meal without some type of beans on the table. He was an astute observer. My mother was not the only bean chef in our family. One of my three Aunt Effies (you know you're from the rural South if you have three Aunt Effies) was known around Hawkins County, Tennessee, for her soup beans. Her full name—as appropriate as one of John Bunyan's characters in *Pilgrim's Progress*—was Effie Kincheloe Bean.

In the rural Tennessee mountain schools of the 1950s, Wednesday was "bean day." The dread of "humpday"—too early in the week to permit the anticipation of the week-end—was always mitigated by the knowledge that the country cooks in our school cafeterias would serve a gourmet bowl of beans with golden brown cornbread for the regular 25-cent cost of lunch. My friends and I would count the minutes until the lunch bell rang. I was teased throughout the school for my feat of eating five or six large bowls of soup beans: the number was restricted only by the short time allotted for lunch. The enthusiasm for bean day was shared by the entire student body and was a significant aspect of our school and community culture, matched only by the flatulence that filled the air of Wednesday afternoon classes. Visiting rural elementary schools in Sullivan County,

Tennessee, only a few years after I had moved away, I observed that the bean day tradition was long dead. The influence of McDonald's and other fast food outlets had already worked to replace bean day with hamburger day, pizza day, and taco day.

The conflicted premodern rural place produced a conflicted consciousness. There was no room for indifference. I loved many aspects of my extended family's world: the kinship ties, the laughter, the physical beauty of the mountains, the stories from previous generations, the humility, and, of course, the cuisine. My negative feelings were equally passionate. I hated the intolerance that expressed itself among many (certainly not all) as a virulent hatred of African Americans and the civil rights movement taking shape around us. I was uncomfortable with the insularity, the reluctance to experience the world outside the comfortable mountain place. Thus, like most of my generation of mountain youth, caught between the premodern past and the exploding modernity around us, I became exceedingly restless. My love–hate relationship with the mountain culture, my "dialectic of place," was ready to engage an institution like McDonald's.

The dialectic was well represented by the symbol of the beans and the McBurgers. On a multiple choice text constructed just for me, one question would read:

Beans are to McBurgers as:

   a) Sunday school is to rock 'n' roll
   b) the Civil War is to Vietnam
   c) Baptist vs. Southern Methodist theological debates are to critical theory vs. existentialism
   d) the daily devotional magazine the *Upper Room* is to *Rolling Stone*
   e) all of the above.

Naturally, *e* is the correct answer.

The dialectic was extremely painful and haunts me until this day. It is merely cliché to observe that writing is nurtured and generated by the discomfort produced by such an abrasive grain of metaphorical sand. Some writers experience conflict between their grand humanitarian impulses and the violent acts they commit to achieve the status of a decorated war hero; my conflict is the lowly clash between the bean and the burger. In this humbling context I am reminded of the realization that one of my greatest "natural" talents was bowling. While this is not the gift needed to play second base for the Detroit Tigers, become a famous blues pianist, assume the status of the hillbilly Kerouac, or burst on the scene as the greatest social comic since Lenny Bruce, I accept my lot: beans versus burgers and picking up the 7–10 split.

The love–hate dialectic continued to inflict its psychic discomfort. I recall sitting in the McDonald's parking lot after a rock band gig in May 1967. With my Farfisa organ and Fender Super Reverb amplifier loaded in my parents' 1962 pink Rambler, I ate my French fries and watched an encounter between a group of "hicks" and four or five upper-middle-class "preppies," as they would be labeled by subsequent generations. As the lower-socioeconomic-class kids pushed and taunted the frightened privileged kids, I understood the anger and hurt that motivated the hicks to get even. Though operating outside any high school clique, I was emotionally connected to the lower-class outsiders. These were the bean-eaters, and though I could never simply fit into their everyday lives, I would carry their hurt with me the rest of my life. It was the same hurt I saw in my father's eyes when he encountered the emerging Tennessee culture of modernity. The primary relationships of premodern mountain life were fading:

everything/everybody was a secondary relationship regulated by a prescribed role.

My McDonald's parking-lot-realization reflected my awkward social location. I was too class-conscious, angry, and hick-inscribed to fit into the modern upwardly mobile group, too reflective and intellectually ambitious to fit in with the premodern toughs, and too familiar and friendly with an agrarian premodern mindset to fit seamlessly into the emerging postmodern counterculture that was creeping into Tennessee and seeping into my consciousness via my knowledge of rock 'n' roll. As I held the small, white package of fries—this was long before the big, red supersized variety had appeared—the understanding began to take shape that my identity was to be found precisely in the consciousness of not belonging. Alas, there was something disturbingly aesthetic, symbolically rich, about the bloodstains discoloring the starched Gant shirts of the popular upper-middle-class boys as they struggled to get back to their new Mustang. My hillbillies were "opening fire" on their tormentors in the quaint way high school revenge played out in the decades before Columbine. Indeed, it was a ritual of revenge that took place time and again in the McDonald's parking lot.

My "not belongingness" became increasingly apparent as the final months of my high school life drifted quickly away. To Aunt Effie and my extended family, my developing knowledge of the music scene and concerns about civil rights, class oppression, and the malignities of patriarchy seemed almost haughty and certainly remote from the travails of their workaday lives. My premodern interpersonal openness—learned from my father's unalienated world of primary relationships—was perceived by my thoroughly modern peers, teachers, and (in adulthood) bosses and supervisors as insincerity at best and a signifier of weakness at worst. My consciousness of such impulses did not destroy my relationships with my hillbilly cultural brothers and sisters, but those impulses moved them to treat me gingerly. Though convinced of my knowledge of their mountain cultural capital and genuine appreciation of them as friends, they knew something about me was a little askew. Because they could not quite put their finger on what it was, I assumed in their eyes the role of enigma.

By the end of high school, my consciousness of these intersecting cultural logics began to reshape my perception of the Golden Arches. My original view had been constructed by the struggle to come to terms with the embarrassment of my origins in light of McDonald's: It represented the modernist validation I sought. As the need for such confirmation faded, I began to see McDonald's with a degree of interpretive distance. The postmodern kernel of my consciousness pushed an increasingly ironic view; my references to "McDonald's" were replaced by a lilting pronunciation of "the Golden Arches." McDonald's was indeed the repository of the modernist capital I had once desired, but I came to the hip realization that—as was true of many things modernist—once possessed, I did not want it at all.

Hamburger Fantasies: McDonald's and the Public Imagination

From teen zines to Internet chat rooms, private thoughts about McDonald's become public knowledge in the contemporary electronic era. As "Burger Queen" writes in the McSpotlight (an anti-McDonald's website), her disdain for the Golden Arches is not political, as the website organizers had hoped, but aesthetic. McDonald's burgers, she maintains:

taste unlike any meat I have tasted. Compare [McDonald's]
burgers to 100% Beefsteaks—not really similar are they? The
buns have as much taste as cotton wool—heavily processed,
no relation to real bread. The whole meal is excessively salty.
I could go on but others have made these points in the past.
(Burger Queen, 1999)

Burger Queen is correct—these points have been made in
the McSpotlight debate room thousands of times. Mike
Bacon (1999) complains that he received a cold burger at
McDonald's three times in a row, while other debaters chime
in with their own tales of aesthetic woe under the Arches.
Reading hundreds of these conversations, I could not help
but be fascinated by how much the debaters care about the
quality (or lack of such) of McDonald's products and how
detailed are their descriptions of the low-quality cuisine in
question. I am also struck by the passion McDonald's supporters bring to their defense of the firm. Why study
McDonald's? Because people care about it so much.

So popular are McDonald's promotions that collectors of
Happy Meal toys have established their own website to
share "Unofficial McDonald's Happy Meal Information" (Toy
Zone, 1999).(McDonald's itself runs the "Official Happy
Meals Web Site.") Discovering the unofficial site, I was
intrigued by the prospect of uncovering "underground" or
maybe countercultural knowledge. The unofficial site grants
Happy Meal toy collectors "secret ways" to obtain their
treasures. Of particular worth to the collector is the large
cardboard display each store gets to advertise the toy accompanying the Happy Meals. There are so many collectors
these days, the webmasters tell their audience, that these
promotional displays are extremely difficult to obtain. Some
outlet managers choose to destroy them because of the
"unpleasant situations" that result when "aggressive collec-

tors" compete for them. Other managers keep the items themselves or give them to favored employees. The secret knowledge the webmasters offer their readers to help them get their hands on these sacred promotions is simple: Get a job at McDonald's (Toy Zone, 1999).

These McDonaphiles are apparently willing to take a low-paying, intensive-labor job to pursue their collecting passion. Collecting the Happy Meal toys is a little easier, apparently not requiring a career change. The experts maintain that "anyone can easily build an impressive collection" of toys "featuring their favorite movie, TV, cartoon or related heroes." Obtaining the colorful boxes and sacks the toys come in may be a bit more difficult, but the toys themselves can be bought at flea markets, swap meets, antique shows, QVC, and house and garage sales. For 30 dollars one can purchase the frequently updated McDonald's Happy Meal collectibles price guide. Indeed, several publications cater to the growing numbers of collectors, and the McDonald's Collector's Club holds an annual convention every April where toys can be brought, traded, and admired (Toy Zone, 1999).

The Sign of the Burger: McDonald's and the American Dream

The Golden Arches won the early battles of the burger wars by transmuting hamburgers into symbols of the post–World War II multileveled mobility and optimism of American life. When Americans discuss McDonald's in everyday conversations, Internet debate rooms, or Happy Meal toy fairs, they are analyzing, praising, criticizing, and questioning themselves. As the hyper-successful epitome of the American Dream, McDonald's corporate iconography attracts meanings like a giant symbolic magnet. Using such significations

McDonald's has played a central role in moving American expenditures on fast food from six billion dollars in 1970 to over 100 billion by the end of the century (Crescenzo, 1997; Jatkinson, 1998; Schlosser, 1998a). So committed were many of my interviewees to the sanctity of the Golden Arches that they bristled when I asked them to respond to criticisms of McDonald's business practices and social roles:

> Why don't these critics of McDonald's go live in Russia or China? They [the critics] don't want to see anybody succeed. They just want a big government to come in and tax away all profits and give the money to the minorities and other people who don't want to work. That man who started the company, Kroc, is an American hero. He was a builder and this country needs more builders. What we don't need are more critics. (Glenn, interview, 1998)

Symbol Migration: The Golden Arches Span the Globe

Outgrowing the borders of the United States, McDonald's has become a truly global enterprise. In this transnational process, the Golden Arches are the symbol of Western economic development—often the first foreign corporation to penetrate a particular nation's market. The Indian social critic Vandana Shiva (1997) found dark humor in the symbol of the Golden Arches. They suggest, she speculated, that when you walk into McDonald's, you are entering heaven, that the corporation wants people around the world to view "the McDonald's experience" as an immersion in celestial bliss—while they are actually eating junk. In terms reminiscent of the mind-set of the Pentagon and the Central Intelligence Agency, McDonald's executives refer to their movement into foreign markets as the company's "global realization" (Schlosser, 1998b).When statues of Lenin came down in East Germany after reunification, giant statues of Ronald McDonald took their place almost overnight. Driving through that country in the late 1990s, I imagined cartoon bubbles coming out of each Ronald's mouth as the clown proclaimed: "No, Nikita, we buried *you*—the West has won." With about 900 of its 20,000 restaurants located in Germany, McDonald's is far and away the largest restaurant company in the country (Schlosser, 1998b).

"Susan Brown," an African American preschool teacher in South Carolina, recollected her excitement in the mid-1960s about the new McDonald's opening in a nearby town. Susan's parents packed the kids into the car and drove miles to the Golden Arches. Exploding out of the car, Susan and her brothers and sisters ran to enter the restaurant, only to be stopped in the parking lot by the manager, who told her father: "We don't allow niggers in McDonald's." "I will never forget the manager's ironed white shirt and dark tie, how he looked when he spoke to my father. I'll never forget my father putting us back into the car" (interview, 1992).

Hong Kong–born American Mandy Kwan also has a McDonald's story. Hers differs from Susan's in significant ways:

> I grew up in Hong Kong during the 1980s, a time when Western fast food restaurants were beginning to emerge. As a child living in a metropolitan city saturated with advertisements and promotions to entice consumers like me, I grew up with McDonald's, Burger King, Kentucky Fried Chicken, Pizza Hut, and other American franchised restaurants and stores. It was the McDonald's Happy Meals, the self-service salad counter of Pizza Hut, and the "finger-lickin' good" friendly chicken at KFC that lured me. The fact that I am able to have my own meal and to choose the greens I want at Pizza Hut is what appealed to me: to be able to choose and be independent. Eating in an Asian culture is a communal experience; when I can

have my own plate and side orders it is a way to exert my choice into the daily rituals of my life.

Nevertheless, McDonald's was the place that enthralled me. Remembering how my classmates and I took pride in knowing the Big Mac jingle or getting to try the latest burger promoted, McDonald's was always the "cool" place to be. Modern and hip Chinese parents would take a child to fast food restaurants because that signifies an acceptance and an embrace of American capitalism. Hong Kong welcomes fast food with open arms, and large populations are waiting to be entertained and amazed by these franchises.

When I walked into a McDonald's, at the age of eight or nine, I had this indescribable sense of awe and reverence for the place. In the McDonalds in my neighborhood, at the entrance a huge Ronald McDonald figure welcomed and ushered me into a world of make-believe. The place was just so clean and user-friendly! The plastic chairs were so fun to sit on, the round little tables and stools that spin made McDonalds almost like a fantasyland. A section in the restaurant was just reserved for birthday parties; in this corner sat a plastic enchanted talking tree from the forest with the little French fry buddies sitting by this tree friend. I remember that I envied my next-door neighbor who had her birthday party in McDonald's. She had these special gifts and party favors that were exclusively McDonald's—and she was crowned the enchanted forest princess.

I never admitted this to anyone, but I used to save all the wrappers and boxes from the countless Big Macs and cheeseburgers (and sometimes the French fry red boxes too). I brought them home and played McDonald's at home. I would pretend to be a McDonald's cashier or manager, churn up a big happy smile, and say, "How can I help you today? May I please have your order?"

I soon grew out of this childish and materialistic fascination with McDonalds. However, the legacy continues. During a visit to Canton, China, in the summer of 1998, I brought my eight-year-old cousin Yan to McDonald's. This particular McDonald's had been open in that city for nearly a year and was located in a frequently traveled intersection that also housed Western-style clothing stores and various businesses. Yan proudly showed me her collection of Happy Meal toys, ranging from a wind-up French fry boxcar to a soda cup with wheels. Compared to the usual costs of dining out, McDonald's is slightly more expensive than the common eateries, but still affordable. My promise to bring Yan to McDonald's was rewarded by a cheer and a hug from her. She gladly took my hand and we strolled down to the McDonalds. She seemed to know all the nuances of the restaurant: where the napkins are placed, how the straw dispenser works, or where to form a line.

Yan ordered a Happy Meal (not to my surprise) and led me to a place to sit. I watched as she perfectly knew how to unwrap the burger and took a big bite out of it. It was rather sloppy to see her eat this way—but who cares? We have all the napkins we can get in the world. She may perhaps be learning the Western ways and cultures of eating, but definitely she is consuming the American idea of waste and overconsumption of materials. One can imagine the papers that go to waste in a typical fast food meal. She also enjoyed the same "self-autonomy" that I experienced when I ordered my own meals. Yan was also up-to-date with the latest promotions of McDonald's; she orders for her parents when they go to the restaurant. It is a child's world, and she loves every second of it. (Interview, 1999)

Why McDonald's? When the Golden Arches Elicit Disdain

As I moved into a more ironic perspective on McDonald's and the modernity it represented, the politics of the corporation and especially those of its founder, Ray Kroc, fascinated me. As the civil rights and the antiwar movements of the 1960s gained momentum, Kroc went on the offensive. Projecting an "America, love it or leave it" message, he frequently denounced the "non-conformists" circulating in America during the era. Referring to demonstrations against McDonald's business and environmental policies, Kroc wrote in his autobiography: "What these fanatics actually opposed was the capitalist system. Their political cant held that to be successful in the context of free enterprise, a business must be morally corrupt and guilty of all kinds of shabby business practices. I feel sorry for people who have such a small and wretched view of the system that made this country great" (Kroc, 1977, p. 180). With such pronouncements and his explicit identification of McDonald's as an institution that fully supported the war in Vietnam, Kroc insured decades of countercultural disdain for the corporation. Such a cultural divide continues to play out. In Internet chat rooms, countless debates can be monitored between conscientious McDonald's managers and countercultural critics. In the course of a circuitous argument, "Luke Kuhn," a member of the Utopian Anarchist Party, writes about initiating disruption at a particular McDonald's. The following exchange takes place:

> *Manager:* Umm . . . I have one thing to say . . . any shit happens in our store, we call the state police . . . I repeat anything. I am the manager at my McDonald's and that's our policy. So how many state cops do you want to arrest you? To anyone who decides to try that, to the author of this . . . Grow the Hell up!

> *Luke:* You better watch who you call the pigs on. Since you always call them, it would be a simple matter to filter a large number of demonstrators in ordinary dress and without signs into the store, then have a few "marked" demonstrators invade the store and let you call the cops. When they arrive, ALL the demonstrators erupt from their seats and fight the cops to defeat them. (Kuhn, 1999)

Thanks to its extraordinary and expensive efforts over the decades to connect itself to a traditional notion of America and conservative American values, McDonald's has become a lightning rod for progressive critiques. As some people in America and many around the world maintain, McDonald's makes an excellent symbol for American cultural and economic imperialism. In the city of Santos, Brazil, several schoolteachers told me that they were worried about the impact of McDonald's on their pupils. One teacher told me: "The danger of McDonald's imperialism is that it teaches children to devalue Brazilian things and to believe that the U.S. is superior to all of us poor South Americans" (interview, 1997). The anger these women directed at the Golden Arches was inscribed on each word they spoke. In the same context many of the women who attended the 1995 Beijing Women's Conference said that one of the highlights of the event was the demonstration against the McDonald's outlet at the Non-Governmental Organization (NGO) Forum. As Vandana Shiva describes it:

> . . . the protest really was an initiative of the younger women at a lecture I was giving on food security, intellectual property rights and biodiversity, and was basically just talking about how the control over the food system is shifting, through various mechanisms, into the hands of a few corporations.
>
> And one of the young women stood up and said: "Did you know that Ronald McDonald is here without a visa? Do you think he should be here?" I said well if they can make such a fuss about the Tibetans not getting visas I think we should make a lot of fuss about Ronald McDonald here without the permission of the NGO Forum—after all McDonald's is not an NGO! What's it doing in the NGO Forum?
>
> The younger women started the march and asked if I would join and I was only too happy to join. We basically took the Ronald McDonald image, which I find gross and obscene, and grows in size all over the world—I really have the urge after Beijing to pull it down wherever I go and sit on it.
>
> And we really had discussion[s] with the women from different countries, expressing what it means to them—expressing how it's a symbol of cultural imperialism, it's a symbol of

ecological colonization, and it's a symbol of the pretence of
food that is really a health hazard. (Shiva, 1997)

Progressive, left-wing political anger is directed against
the Golden Arches in the United States and especially overseas. But other anti-McDonald's dynamics also demand
analysis. Much of the public conversation about McDonald's
in the United States possesses a strong elitist current and a
condescension that grants a measure of cultural capital to
those who express it. The last thing I want to do is defend
the culinary value of McDonald's food, but many of the
pronouncements concerning the aesthetics of McDonald's
are excessive. After the appearance of the Arch Deluxe in
1996, several Arch Deluxe Hate Pages appeared on the
Internet. "Arch Deluxe Hate Mail" (1997–) received numerous hits, and scores of people wrote in to express vehement
disdain for the doomed Arch Deluxe:

> *Ian:* I don't have any ad material for you, but I'd like to share
> our nickname for this monstrosity—"The Butt Deluxe." So
> named for its ass-crack emblazoned bun as well as its effect on
> one's digestive tract.

> *Jesters of Burger King's Royal Court:* We love your Arch Deluxe
> Hate Mail page and we're wondering if you [would] like to
> join a plot to assassinate Ronald McDonald?

> *M.K.:* Hello fellow Arch Deluxe hater. We have a neighbor we
> call . . . Arch Deluxe. . . . He is an evil alien from the planet,
> Happy hamburger shit. We, like you, hate McDonald's new
> Arch Deluxe. We have done scientific research, the Arch
> Deluxe stunts growth of major organs. Therefore disproving
> the theory of the grownup taste. I guess they will run out of
> secret sauce soon.

> *Brack:* I, being a dung beetle, am pleased with the new selec-
> tions at McDonald's. I no longer have to hang out in pastures
> to mate. I just go to McDonald's, purchase the reverse enema

deluxe, and roll it into a ball to attract a mate. (Arch Deluxe Hate Mail, 1997)

Underlying the words of many individuals I talked to in person or in cyberspace was a class-inscribed contempt for people who eat and work at McDonald's. So much a part of everyday life is McDonald's for many youths that they find it hard to believe that some people do not know everything about the institution. For example, "Philip," assuming the role of an amateur ethnographer, observed McDonald's customers in all their ineptitude:

> You would think these folks, often spending a considerable amount of time in a lengthy line, would have had a moment or two to gather their thoughts and be prepared with an order once they had moved to the front of the line. You would think but you would be wrong. These poor, unfortunate souls would step up to the counter to order and then stare all puzzled-like at the menu, as if they had wandered into the wrong fast food franchise by mistake. They would cock their heads—the universal symbol of "I have no idea what I'm about to order" and then pester the pimply-faced, lard-assed teenagers manning the counter with a bunch of useless questions.

Philip continues with a cognitive analysis of McDonald's customers:

> I'm sorry, placing an order at McDonald's does not require this level of intellectual involvement. There are not that many choices to wrestle with. You can have hamburgers with cheese or without. You can have a large size of fried products or a smaller size. You do not have to debate the merits of pork versus chicken (unless we're talking about the McRib versus the McChicken Deluxe variety), you do not have to wonder whether the white or red wine goes with the Filet O'Fish, you do not have to ask the clerk why Mayor McCheese is no longer featured in the TV commercials and when are you guys going to get around to suing Barney-the-Dinosaur people for infringing on that Grimace copyright.

. . . a woman sauntered up to the counter and actually asked the following question: "Yeah, how does your two chicken sandwiches for $2 work?" Um. Let me see if I can explain this ma'am. You see in our society money can be exchanged for goods or services. In the olden days under the barter system, you would have to bring something that I need—say, a really good axe—and trade it for my chicken sandwiches. But that grew to be complicated, so we developed a system where money—that is to say, printed paper regarded as legal tender—can instead be used. And if you were to give me two dollars, then I would, in turn, give you two chicken sandwiches. And I would be sure to poison them to preclude the possibility of you breeding and passing along your clearly congenital stupidity to your hapless spawn. ("Philip," 1996)

In this elitist context I detected a virulent anger toward McDonald's employees that moved Philip's condescending reference to "pimply-faced, lard-assed teenagers" to a new level. Writing in the hacker and cyberpunk *Phrack Magazine*, Charlie X (1994) suggests a set of anti-McDonald's actions that seem to be aimed more at hurting low-level employees than the corporation. The following prank is directed at the employee who takes out the garbage:

GARBAGE CAN TRICKS

Since McDonald's is usually a busy restaurant, the trash bags fill up quickly and must be changed frequently (but never are). For starters, ask for hot or boiling water. If you don't want to attract attention by doing this, bring in your own really hot water . . . boil it, put it in a Styrofoam cup or a thermos. . . . once in McDonald's, locate the filled trash can (should not be hard to find) and dump the hot water down the side. Not only will this melt the side of the bag, causing the trash to go everywhere, the person who takes out the garbage must pick up all the trash by hand and dump out the trash can with water in the bottom. This also soaks the trash, breaks up paper, and makes the whole experience quite unpleasant, but hilarious to watch. (1994, n.p. [p. 2])

"Food Tricks" is designed to get the cooks into trouble:

There are several things to do with the food. Since there is
probably something wrong with it in the first place, you might
want to simply make the problem bigger. . . . Before you enter
the restaurant, cut some of your hair, or hair off of a pet.
When at your table, place the hair all over the inside of the
burger. When the line at the counter is long and everyone is
busy, cut up to the front of the counter, and start complaining
about your burger. Show EVERYONE the hair inside the
burger. You will get another burger, and most likely, a lot of
free shit so you will come back. You will also cause most
everyone to leave, and people in the kitchen to get shit on by
the manager.

"On a Busy Day" gives advice on hassling the counter
employees:

Busy days are the best. Customers are in a hurry, so are the
employees . . . everyone has a short fuse and usually do not
pay attention to what you say, or get very pissed. Ask for real
dumb shit. . . . For example, "I'd like a 69 piece Chicken
McNugget." The best thing to do is to order a simple cheeseburger and screw it all up with special orders. . . . For example,
I'd like a cheeseburger, with extra cheese, no mustard, extra
catsup, extra onions, lettuce, tomato, a real little dab of mayo,
and make it well done . . . oh wait, I don't want cheese anymore. Just put extra lettuce on it . . . [wait for them to send
the order back to the kitchen] . . . then "Oh, wait, sorry . . . I
just want a Big Mac." You can also say, "I'd like a medium
Coke with just 4 pieces of ice in it." They will always do what
you say. . . . Keep in mind that special orders do not cost extra,
so you can order a hamburger, ask for extra mustard, catsup,
and somewhere in there, casually mention extra cheese . . . 9
times out of 10 this works . . . and you don't get charged.
NOTE: if you hear a printer printing followed by 3 beeps somewhere in the kitchen, your grill order was printed, and will be
made . . . so change it after you hear that.

Another suggestion is aimed at the employee working the drive-through window:

DRIVE-THRU FUN

McDonald's videos tell the employees that the Drive Thru makes up for more than 40% of the average McDonald's business. Simply put, this system needs a lot of work. The speakers rarely work, and you usually get your order screwed up. The first thing to do is to take your car and back over the cut square in the pavement right beside the order sign several times. This causes a loud annoying "bong" to be heard by everyone with a headset . . . eventually the manager will come out with a weapon, and this is where you leave. (Charlie X, 1994, n.p.)

As I attempt to answer the "Why McDonald's?" question, the desire to harm the *employees* of a socially irresponsible corporation baffles me. Is it political naiveté that keeps Charlie X and scores like him from separating the corporate culprits from their victims, their underpaid and exploited labor force? I was surprised by the Internet popularity of Charlie X's essay, which was reprinted and referenced in numerous cyber-venues.

Is the Progressive Critique of McDonald's Elitist?

As a progressive concerned with social justice, the abuses of corporate power, and equity, I listened to many of my interviewees and read the works of activists such as Charlie X with trepidation. On some level they resented the corporate power McDonald's has amassed, but many of them wanted to tell me about the time some wretched employee mistakenly substituted a Quarter Pounder for a Big Xtra, greeted them impolitely, or made them wait for their food. Would such an attitude be perceived as the progressive position?

Would the views of cultural workers trying to salvage public democracy from corporate power plays be dismissed as a condescending elitism? There is, much to my anguish, enough elitism to be uncovered within the academic left—among scholars of cultural studies in particular. Indeed, one of the reasons for the failure of progressive politics over the last 30 years is the popular association of the American left with condescension toward working people.

While McSpotlight represents an island of hope in a sea of neo-liberal and neo-conservative corporate politics, reading the debate pages mitigated my optimism. As the avowed anti-McDonaldite Jay responds to a McDonald's manager, condescension permeates his words. The manager had asserted that he provides a social service:

> Please tell me kind and witty sir, just what good you think you do for people on a daily basis (leaving out, for now, your priceless contributions to current sociological theory via stinging and cunning polemics)? And do tell how you think the inescapable presence of McDonald's in this world is supposed to help me along in my morning? Is it supposed to repulse me that I have no option other than to completely succumb to an overwhelming existential crisis, the likes of which shall whisk me away from pre-reflective thought to a fuller self-consciousness? ("Jay W.," 1999)

Responding to a McDonald's employee, anti-McDonaldite Tony Tiger ridicules McWorkers' tendency to take the money they earn and buy a "new Plymouth, make payments, and think they are doing a grand job of living the dream of the American Hamburglar" (1999). No one can miss the condescending class bias pulsating in his statement. This approach pushes McDonald's workers into the arms of the corporation. Where else are they to go? To a left that seems to have no more concern for them than corporate farms do for their migrant workers? Corporate leaders at least pretend to respect their employees. We're honorable people, McDonald's employees contend; show us some respect. "I take pride in my job and maintain an allegiance to my company," one interviewee said (1998). "I believe such loyalty will be rewarded." This woman saw the progressive critique of McDonald's as an elitist position and a personal insult. An Australian McDonald's manager writes with these concerns in mind. The reader can sense how elitist critics have pushed him into his current position:

> I honestly would not want another job. I love working for McDonald's. It has proven to be a great career move for me and I continue to learn skills that most of you idiots would have no idea about. Not all McDonald's people are stupid. If you believe that all of the several million people who work for this great company are morons, then perhaps you should really look at who is pointing the finger. It is a fallacy that all crew people are slaves and are treated like dogs. My crew love coming to work, it is social and rewarding. ("Store Manager," 1999)

Although I am acutely aware of the political problems with this statement, I recognize the manager's hurt in the same way I understood the motivations of my hick friends who jumped the popular high school boys in the Kingsport McDonald's parking lot in 1967.

Proclamations like those of the Australian manager are numerous. "Kati" (1999) asserts that she is sick and tired of those elite bastards who "think that because you work at McDonald's that your IQ is somewhere around 10 and that you can't complete a thought without help from the aliens who implanted that chip when I was 8." Her complaint reflects the feelings of scores of other McDonald's employees who tell the anti-McDonald's people to "go shove your

nose up your arse . . . and stop hassling us, we're only trying to earn a living" ("Gromit," 1999). My research indicates
that a large number of McDonald's employees automatically associate political criticism of the company with disdain
for them and their low-status position. Although more
mature and thoughtful anti-McDonald's activists studiously
avoid that position, many do not. The impact of such elitism
on the social perceptions and political consciousness of
many workers is tragic.

Thus, as a result of twists in the postmodern condition,
some working people see the left as their enemy. "You
vicious people" who put us down, one worker pleads, "save
your breath because I will not waste my time defending
myself" ("Jen," 1999). The alienation McDonald's workers
feel often moves them to create their own subculture with
informal support systems. Many design T-shirts for fellow
employees with inside jokes imprinted on them. One
employee gave her fellow crew members shirts adorned
with "The Top Ten Most Irritating Things That Really Burn
My Ass About Working Drive Thru Service." When her
workmates saw the list, she reported, they laughed until
they cried ("Jen," 1999). One detects a Zen-like effort to deal
with the lack of respect, as employees counsel one another
that they can't change the situation but they can modify
how it affects them emotionally ("Sharon," 1999). Sometimes exasperated workers explicitly aim the "Why McDonald's?" question at their elite detractors. Several employees
I interviewed responded to left attacks by asking: "Why the
hell are you picking on McDonald's? You're probably working for a corrupt corporation too."

2 Hugging McDonald's

The McDonald's folks have gained a edge by making you want to hug them....At my inner city yuppie McDonald's a few nights back, a young lawyer ahead of me pointed out to the cashier that she had undercharged him by $1.87. "Your mom would be proud of you," I joked with him. "Aw, I couldn't cheat McDonald's," he replied. "It'd be like stealing from Mickey Mouse."
— Penny Moser, "The McDonald's Mystique," *Fortune*, July 4, 1994, p. 115

McDonald's ideological work has been so successful that it, like Disney, has taken on an identity that positions it beyond criticism in the public conversation. Many members of the American public have given their consent to the corporate agenda of free enterprise economics—an agenda that positions the rights of property and commerce over the best interests of the community, values the dictates of the market over the democratic process, and maintains that there is no connection between the ownership and economic interests of the media and the globalized corporate world. As one of the customers waiting in a long line for the new Beanie Baby told me:

McDonald's means everything to my son and me. My husband left us a few years ago and it's just me and my son now. I work different shifts over at the hospital and don't have much time to cook. I hate what the government does to us working people, taxing us to pay for those welfare loafers. If it wasn't for McDonald's I'd probably be on welfare too. I'd never accept it, mind you. I truly love McDonald's and what they stand for. I love those Beanie Babies too. My son and I have all of them.

He won't eat my cooking any more; he'd rather have a Big
Mac. (Peggy, interview, 1996)

The Nature of Ideology

If the public consents to such precepts, then why shouldn't
they want to hug McDonald's and the other providers of the
good life? One inclined to do so has probably been affected
at some level by the ideology of McDonald's and its corporate allies. Dominant ideology makes inequality appear to be
the inevitable outcome of the economic elite's superior talent and effort. Even though the term "ideology" is used in
a variety of ways, two categories of use prevail. The first
usage involves ideology as a set of political beliefs, as in the
ideology of a political party, drawn upon for the construction
of policies and platforms. Under this definition ideologies
come to be thought of as "isms"—Marxism, liberalism, con-
servatism, libertarianism, and so on. Conceptualizing ideology in this manner causes problems, as it conveys two
misconceptions regarding power. First, seeing ideology as a
system of beliefs held by politically oriented groups and
individuals clouds our view of the ways ideology operates in
our lives through cultural pedagogy, advertising, and interpersonal relations. Second, this definition presents ideology
as a static phenomenon removed from the cultural context
in which it always operates.

The way in which beliefs are acted upon (many use the
term "mobilized") is central to a critical understanding of ideology. Certain ways of seeing the world may work to sustain
existing power relations in one context but undermine them
in another. In order to understand the continually shifting
contextual dynamics in the culture of power, we need to
move beyond the definition of ideology as a coherent system

of beliefs and develop a more complex, process-oriented, culturally sensitive approach. Such a definition would address ideology in its dominant guise as part of a larger process of protecting unequal power relations, of maintaining domination. Specifically, a dominant cultural form of ideology involves sustaining these power asymmetries through the process of making meaning, producing a common sense that justifies prevailing systems of domination. The comments of the working mother in the Beanie Baby line revealed an ideological dynamic: Government was bad, rewarding the unworthy via welfare payments; McDonald's was good, providing fast, low-cost meals that children like. Such a perception induces particular forms of political behavior. When I asked the woman if she would mind telling me her political affiliation, she said: "Most of the time I vote for the man, but I guess I'm a Republican. I'm definitely not one of them liberals like Kennedy." Ideology theory was invented in the first place to explain why individuals from the lower socioeconomic class in industrialized societies continued to support the political and economic systems that exploited them or, later, to explain why many women seemed to accept patriarchal domination. A critical conception of ideology finds its grounding in this traditional democratic concern with the maintenance of power disparity, taking very seriously the contextually sensitive aspects of meaning-making that accompany it. When such contextual dynamics are viewed as a cardinal aspect of ideology, then we can begin to appreciate the insidious ways power operates in the culture at large and in institutions.

Ideology cannot be separated from our understanding of hegemony. Hegemony involves the maintenance of domination, not through force, but through winning the consent of the individuals being dominated. If hegemony is the larger effort of the powerful to win the consent of their "subordinates," then dominant or, better, hegemonic ideology involves the cultural forms, meanings, rituals, and representations that produce consent to the status quo and individuals' particular places within it. Hegemonic consent is never completely established, as various groups with different agendas always contest it. Looking at ideology in terms of hegemony moves us beyond the simplistic explanations that use terms like "propaganda" to describe the ways in which media, cultural pedagogy, and other cultural productions coercively manipulate citizens to adopt oppressive patterns of meaning. The proponents of what could be labeled hegemonic ideology understand a much more subtle and ambiguous form of domination and reject the propaganda model's assumption that its subjects are passive, manipulable victims. Students of hegemonic consent understand that dominant ideological practices and discourses socially construct our vision of reality (Deetz, 1993; Fiske, 1993; Kellner, 1990; McLaren, 1994; Thompson, 1987).

In this ideological context, this culture of power, McDonald's can produce great loyalties and validate particular ways of thinking. In an interview with an Indonesian national living temporarily in the United States, I asked how he reacted to the first McDonald's opening in Jakarta. "I was very proud," he replied. He derived a personal sense of validation from McDonald's decision to locate in the city. "We had become something more than we previously had been," he concluded. "We had been chosen by McDonald's" (interview, September 6, 1998). I remembered when Kingsport, Tennessee, had been chosen, in 1962. Other observers (e.g., Caputo, 1998) have referred to this validation process, connecting it to a sense of worthiness to participate in the American Dream. The ideology of McDonald's conjures a number of positive images that consumers attach to themselves in the act of consumption.

The Ideology of McDonald's

Those of us who explore the ideology of McDonald's are not asserting that CEOs Michael Quinlan and Jack Greenberg and the corporation's upper management are secretly conspiring to overthrow democracy and control the world as we know it. This is where many people miss the meaning of ideology and misunderstand how it operates. One young man read my critique of McDonald's ideological power in *Kinderculture: The Corporate Construction of Childhood* (Steinberg and Kincheloe, 1997) and responded:

> I just don't get it. People like you are scared of hamburgers and running shoes. McDonald's is just a company that sells hamburgers. Nike is just a company that sells shoes. They are not conspiring together to take over the world. I think all of you conspiracy buffs are paranoid. Ronald McDonald is just a clown—he's not even real. McDonald's has power because it makes money selling people what they want. (Interview, 1998)

Many people with whom I spoke held the same opinion: Power is easy to identify; nothing that is invisible to the naked eye is taking place in this political domain. They miss the occluded and complex nature of the culture of power. McDonald's is an ideological power agent, making social and cultural meanings in its pursuit of economic goals that can be attained only in the context of existing power relations. That is: McDonald's, in pursuing business as usual and in employing particular marketing strategies, operates as an ideological agent (Goldman and Papson, 1996). Consider the important ways this process takes place.

Constructing a World

McDonald's and other corporate meaning-makers market a world where the unfettered free enterprise system produces nothing but freedom and satisfaction for consumer citizens. Erased from this corporately constructed cosmos is the reality in which the interests of low-wage fast food workers and those of private property owners and mega-profiteers collide, often in ugly ways. Drawing upon "paleosymbols" that signify significant human relationships—the love of family and place—and the pleasure and security that come with them, McDonald's advertising portrays scenes that are common to the experience of most viewers. To construct an ideological world, the company reflects the emotions of everyday life, depicting, for example, a little sister running to catch up with a big brother as the scene fades to the Golden Arches. The paleosymbol of sibling relationships is mobilized in McDonald's interest; in the process McMarketers suture the values and emotional investments of private experience to the ideology of consumerism, free market economics, and corporate legitimation.

As the construction of political consciousness moves to the cultural site of entertainment and advertising, corporate use of paleosymbols and other emotionally charged signifiers undermines political dialogue and shuts off the possibility for analysis of the public issues insidiously referenced in these productions. McDonald's ads, for example, work so well that many find any argument delineating their political significance to be absurd. A hamburger, they will repeat, is just a hamburger.

Any construction of a new world needs a good history. In McDonald's ideological world-making, history is both constructed and robbed of its signifiers to connect consumer desire to the Big Mac. The nostalgic notion of the vague American past as a time of simple virtue, family values, and happiness is consistently grafted onto a company that did not exist in that nebulous past. The memories of the local raconteur, the family genealogist, and (with globalization) the tribal griot are co-opted and replaced by the antiqued film of McDonald's history. It is both fascinating and disconcerting to observe this process taking place among children watching McDonald's ads on television. The memories important in their lives are not those of grandparents but those fabricated by McDonald's and other corporate history-makers. McDonald's antiqued film version of small-town America destroys any sense of shared history, transforming it into privatized myth, a generic symbol of "past." In the hands of McMarketers, this generic past becomes something McDonald's works to protect for all of us. Once again ideology has undermined sociohistorical understanding and mobilized a simulated meaning to serve the corporate interest. Using grainy black and white or faded color film, McDonald's transubstantiates history into myth. Take, watch ye all of this in the name of Kroc the father, Ronald the son, and the McDonald's corporate spirit. We go to prepare a better world for you (Deetz, 1993; Goldman and Papson, 1996).

The corporate process of world-making via the construction of history (or histories) is a spectacle: the McDonald's small town, Dean Witter admonishing his employees, Maxwell House's 1892 Fourth of July parade, Disney's romanticization of California life in the 1950s. The list goes on. Another aspect of McDonald's ideological world-making involves the construction of a corporate origin myth. Indeed, the very creation of McDonald's makes meaning: Kroc the capitalist genius emerged one fateful day in 1954 in the San Bernadino desert from the cocoon of Kroc the traveling milkshake-mixer salesman. When he first laid eyes on Dick and Mac McDonald's restaurant, the new, metamorphosed, and inspired Kroc may have exclaimed, "Behold, I have seen the future." Only Joel and Ethan Coen could do cinematic justice to this scene. Verily, Kroc's future could be expressed in one sacred word—franchising.

In the widely known and ideology-packed McDonald's origin myth, 50-something-year-old Ray Kroc, the washed-up milkshake-mixer salesmen, becomes the auteur of hamburger marketing and franchising. Creative and independent, with a Jimmy Cagney—like pugnacity and an inferiority-inspired bravado, Kroc the father (or, as he liked to call himself, Big Daddy) metaphorically dispensed a piece of himself on every burger: two all-beef patties, special sauce, lettuce, cheese, onions, pickles, ideology, and Kroc himself on a sesame-seed bun? In the semiotic dimension, the Big Mac gets bigger and bigger. As the Kroc-owned McDonald's began to prosper, the media seized the Kroc image and the McDonald's myth. Kroc was quickly placed among the pantheon of corporate managers and garnered the media adulation reserved for men in that category—Iacocca, Trump, the pre-presidential-candidate Perot, Virgin's Richard Branson, and Rupert Murdoch. McDonald's did not have to publicize its historical mythology; television, radio, and the print media were all too glad to do so.

Kroc parlayed his story to the media as a saga of entrepreneurial ingenuity supported by the ideology of free enterprise. Business magazines turned him and his McDonald's into holy icons—*Fortune* speaks of him as a papal figure patting us on the head and blessing us for playing McDonald's Monopoly game (Moser, 1994). Residents of Downey in southern California held McDonald's history so sacred that they expressed outrage when the company decided to tear down what was in 1993 the third-oldest operating McDonald's. Described as a "pre-Kroc" landmark," the restaurant, built in August 1953, elicited pledges from town leaders and citizens that they would eat a designated number of "hamburgers, fries, drinks, and breakfast items" to keep it open. "Pre-Kroc landmark"—it sounds like the postmodern equivalent of a pre-Columbian artifact. The Downeyites display an acceptance of the ideological origin myth that is disconcerting. Have the ideological campaigns of the commodified privatized realm so disrupted meaning-making that McDonald's has become the most treasured historical artifact on the southern California landscape? A process of historical erasure is taking place not only in Downey, California, but also in the United States and now the world in general. In order to create a world, another world has to be destroyed. As Ronald McDonald pushes Uncle Sam aside, Kroc and his McDonald's outlets replace a host of historical figures and artifacts (Deetz, 1993; du Gay et al., 1997; Goldman and Papson, 1996; Kincheloe, 1999; Moser, 1994; Weinstein, 1993).

Disguising Class Inequality

In a mediated, electronic society, the ideology of corporate legitimation always involves the manipulation of signifiers and images. In this semiotic process a corporation's goal is to subtly, if not subliminally, counter and dismiss criticism from detractors in areas such as labor, environmental politics, racial and gender justice, child advocacy, nutrition, or critical pedagogy. Political images are designed not to stimulate public conversation about an issue, but, conversely, to silence debate. This ideological tactic helps to depoliticize the public and teach them not to think in political terms. Corporate image campaigns reduce political/ideological issues to personal and aesthetic ones, matters of the private (not public) domain. Like the rewriting-of-history ads, these image campaigns speak to "our values," a better time when all these agitators—especially those advocates of race and gender justice—knew to keep quiet.

The class dynamics inscribed by these legitimation signifiers and image campaigns are complex and often ambiguous. While socioeconomic class figures prominently in McDonald's operations, it can never be separated from issues of age, race, gender, and geographic place. The complexity of these class issues is illustrated by McDonald's ability to represent itself to millions of people as the embodiment of democracy and egalitarianism. Everyone is treated equally at McDonald's, whether the restaurant is located in Berlin, Bangkok, Beijing, or Bulls Gap, Tennessee; since the food is standardized, no one is embarrassed by having to order the cheapest item on the menu. I watched this egalitarian feature play out in my own rural East Tennessee upbringing. My father, born in 1905 to a rural farm family in Hawkins County, Tennessee, in the already poor southern Appalachian Mountains, was severely victimized by the great Depression. Both he and my mother worked in the early 1930s, often going months between paychecks. "If you want to keep your job, you'll have to forgo pay this month," employers would tell them. This experience haunted my father until the day he died, making it psychologically difficult for him to spend money. Unneeded spending, he and my mother grew to believe, was a clear sign of moral weakness. Eating out when it was possible to prepare food at home more economically was especially weak.

When a McDonald's opened in 1962 in Kingsport, Tennessee, its advertisements proclaiming 15-cent hamburgers and 12-cent French fries caught my father's attention. When ads touted the price difference between eating at McDonald's and eating at other restaurants, my father was enthralled. To this self-identified working-class man, eating at McDonald's was an act of class resistance. He never cared for the food— he would much rather have eaten my mother's country ham and cornbread. But as we ate the burgers, he spoke at length and with enthusiasm about how McDonald's beat the price of other hamburgers around town by at least 50 or 60 cents. The knowledge gave him great pleasure. Like others in their particular social spaces around the world, my father con-sumed a democratic egalitarian ethos. French teenagers accustomed to the bourgeois stuffiness of French restaurants could have identified with my father's class-resistant con-sumption, as they have reveled over the past 20 years in the perceived informality and freedom of McDonald's "American atmosphere" (Leidner, 1993, p. 222). Socially savvy mar-keters in France have picked up on this dynamic with slogans like: "Be like the Americans, eat at McDonald's."

A similar class dynamic can be observed in McDonald's postmodernesque attack on the haute cuisine of modernist high culture. No member of the cultural avant-garde would be caught dead in a McDonald's, for it is possible to gain cul-tural capital (knowledge that can be used for social mobil-ity and status) via one's consumption of food. Since culinary taste holds class consequences, the cultural vanguard sees dining at McDonald's as the province of the gauche. Kroc was a master at exploiting this aspect of McDonald's, stand-ing up against the elitism of leftist intellectuals and social snobs. Time and again my interviewees praised Kroc and McDonald's antielite populism of the right. In radio inter-views I gave after publishing a chapter on McDonald's in *Kinderculture: The Corporate Construction of Childhood* (Steinberg and Kincheloe, 1997), my critical stance quickly labeled me as a part of the elite left and elicited strident reactions from callers to almost everything I had to say.

Kroc and McDonald's had done a good job of inscribing the democratic populist signifier on the company. My criticisms were perceived by listeners not simply as an attack on McDonald's, but as an attack on them; many in the radio audience thought I was looking down on them, their politics, their aesthetics, and their eating habits. If that had been my intention, they would probably have been right to be angry. How dare that academic snob challenge the democratic ethos that says we all eat at McDonald's as free and equal citizens? Even that damned O. J. Simpson ate at McDonald's the night Nicole was murdered. He and Kato drove his Rolls Royce to the drive-in window and ordered their burgers. Now there's a democratic image of McDonald's in media-driven hyperreality.

Researchers find similar class issues at work around the world. In China, for example, banquets are extremely competitive, and hosts attempt to excel by purchasing the most costly entrees and beverages. A host can be humiliated if diners at a nearby table are consuming a more expensive cuisine. Because of the relative standardization of prices at McDonald's, Chinese hosts of banquets held under the Golden Arches do not have to suffer such anxieties (Yan, 1997).

Obviously these democratic perceptions do not constitute the entire story of McDonald's relation to socioeconomic class. For example, as McDonald's began its major expansion in the 1980s, American body weight began to increase. Poor people in particular have borne the brunt of this increase in weight and fat, as their diet has changed from humble but moderately healthy fare to Big Macs, fries, and Cokes with their high fat or sugar content. The grandchildren of my

Appalachian aunts and uncles do not eat beans and corn-bread any more. Thus, the democratization process is plagued with contradictions: Allen Shelton's (1995) "democratic theater" at McDonald's, where everyone eats the same fare and is expected to bus his or her own table, is juxtaposed with teenage and female employees' experience of the injuries of class. The ability to portray itself as the citadel of democracy while engaging in hostile labor practices, including resistance to union organizing and fighting for subminimum wages for employees (Kovel 1997), is a prime example of McDonald's mastery of ideological disguise (Block, 1992; Caputo, 1998; Kovel, 1997; Yan, 1997).

Hiding Racial Injustice

McDonald's racial history is fascinating in this ideological context. Although the company has worked to present a public image of racial sensitivity, in the 1960s McDonald's management was reluctant to award franchises to African Americans, prompting demonstrations against and boycotts of McDonald's outlets in black neighborhoods. As a result of such activism, black franchise owners and managers were sought, and public relations efforts to court the black community were initiated. These efforts were set back at the corporation's First International Meeting when an upper-level manager gave a speech blasting lazy people who expect something for nothing and are prone to rioting in the streets. The new black contingent of McDonald's operators were incensed by the covert racial antagonism of the speech and in response formed a black employee organization. This small group, along with the only female operator in the company, drafted a letter to Kroc and his top executives enumerating the company's racial problems. In addition to problems of exclusion, the dissident operators complained of management's insensitivity to the needs of black operators and the black community (Boas and Chain, 1976, pp. 151, 183–84; Kroc, 1977, pp. 126–27; Vidal, 1997, p. 40).

McDonald's public relations strategies seem designed more to provide an inclusive facade than to acknowledge and empower African Americans within the organization. Public relations experts brought in to improve McDonald's image in the black community were primarily concerned with perception-related dynamics such as the way blacks viewed Ronald McDonald. One Madison Avenue consultant maintained that the clown's painted face and red Afro wig made Ronald McDonald an acceptable figure in black communities (Love, 1986). Another advisor assured McDonald's executives that his training program for potential black employees would make sure that "racial animosities are washed out of their heads" (Love, 1986, p. 375). Later McDonald's hired the Burrell Advertising Agency, which produced specialized commercials targeted at black audiences. Drawing upon the paleosymbol of family values, Burrell produced a series of ads sentimentally depicting black middle-class family life that played well in the black community (Seiter, 1993). Such images fostered the illusion that McDonald's was especially sensitive to the needs of African Americans. Following up such strategies, McDonald's hired Robert Beavers, an African American, as "the apostle of the golden Arches," in the words of the magazine *Black Enterprise* (1988, p. 86). Employed to rearticulate the company's racial history, Beavers issued public announcements such as: "I'm proud of the legacy of McDonald's and the role that blacks play as a part of the company's history. I'd like my grandchildren to be able to tell their kids that their grandfather played a part in the hamburger wars" (ibid.).

In the late 1980s and early 1990s, McDonald's came up with new strategies in its attempt to win the consent of the American black community. Constructing a role as an agent of the public welfare and the common good, McDonald's relocated ads targeted at African Americans from traditional small-town settings to the urban black 'hood. In 1990 the company released a television ad entitled "Second Chance" in which a black teenager is rescued from gang life by his McJob. Working at the restaurant teaches the young man the age-old American habits of responsibility, elbow grease, teamwork, a subservient smile, and a "good attitude." A detailed examination of the commercial reveals the ideological dynamics of this public relations campaign.

The first image viewers see is Calvin, a black teenager, walking down the street with a casual gait many whites would associate with a "black attitude." His hat is positioned backward on his head, projecting an image perceived by many contemporary white Americans as a "bad-ass black kid." Viewers eavesdrop on two neighborhood black women who are talking about him as he walks by:

> *First woman:* "Isn't that Calvin?"
>
> *Second woman:* "I haven't seen him for a while. I wonder where he's headin'?"
>
> *First woman:* "I heard he got a job."
>
> *Second woman:* "Is that right? Well it's about time he got himself a job."

In the next frame Calvin approaches a group of bigger and more menacing black males hanging out near the gate of a playground. Represented to viewers by their stances and expressions as dangerous gang members, the group reaches out to pull Calvin symbolically and physically into their circle. But Calvin brushes them away with a safe, unthreatening smile. Immediately after escaping the gang's gravitational pull, Calvin moves toward an elderly woman having trouble with her overloaded grocery cart. At first frightened by the approach of a young black male, she is relieved and elated when Calvin helps with her cart. The camera returns to the two neighborhood women, who are still watching the street scene.

> *First woman:* "Now that you mention it, there is something different about him."
>
> *Second woman:* "Just goes to show you can't judge a book by its cover."
>
> *First woman:* "Looks like responsibility's been good for him."
>
> *Second woman:* "Well I'm just glad somebody believed in him enough to give him a chance."
>
> *First woman:* "Wonder where he's working?"

In the next scene Calvin enters McDonald's, immediately turning his cap around to signify his rejection of black street life. In its role as "provider of public welfare," McDonald's has granted Calvin a "second chance." As a member of the McFamily with its traditional American values, Calvin gains the fortitude to reject the criminal life of the black street gang. Regardless of the bad pay and impersonal working conditions, the McDonald's job can produce miracles. Indeed, McDonald's is endowed with an almost mystical power to "save the sinner," to turn surly black street warriors into obsequious counter boys.

> *Smiling Calvin:* "Welcome to McDonald's. May I help you?"

Thus, McDonald's ideological message about race is not merely that it is sensitive to such issues, but that it is a source of hope for the black community. A semiotic reading of "Second Chance" and other ads exposes problematic aspects of McDonald's racial self-representation. "Second Chance" presents a disturbing picture of black youth, implying an inherent criminality and violence that must be tempered by a civilizing agency like McDonald's. The initial depiction of Calvin as a typical African American urban youth is designed to signify his dangerousness. After all, you can't judge a book by its cover, and Calvin's "cover" is bad, threatening, and foreboding. The signifier of the black street gang stereotypes young people in black communities. This is the life for which Calvin is headed without McDonald's civilizing intervention. A casual white observer of the ad will probably experience it as a reinforcement of his or her fear of and discomfort around black youths and the violent role they are perceived to play in society (Goldman and Papson, 1996). In addition to inscribing the ideology of McDonald's as supporter of the public good, "Second Chance" may also serve to exacerbate the racial prejudice of white viewers. And it serves to disguise McDonald's dubious racial history by portraying the company once again as an organization that cares for, and provides another chance for, our black citizens.

McDonald's has received public praise over the last couple of decades for the relative prominence of African Americans, Latinos, and Asians in its television commercials featuring children. A semiotic reading of these "diversity ads," however, reveals more ambiguous ideological issues at work. Lead roles in multiethnic McDonald's commercials still go to "All-American" kids—the ad agency code term for white youngsters. In many of these ads, racial consistencies emerge, all involving a strange visual marginalization of nonwhite kids. In ad after ad black children are stationed in glancing profile or over-the-shoulder shots and at the edge of the camera frame, overtly out of focus. This out-of-focus shot is often used in documentary-style sequences filmed with a hand-held camera that pans rapidly past African American children. In addition to such visual marginalization, young black actors in the commercials set at McDonald's are left out of group discussions about what they want to be when they grow up. The ideological message is encoded that the professional roles of doctors, lawyers, and engineers are reserved for white children. The consistency of these types of representations is disconcerting to those concerned with racial justice.

One of the corporation's longest-running ads presents a simulated history through old photographs interspersed with antiqued film footage of scenes depicting particular moments in American history. A "Greek" chorus sings about the ideological relationship between family values and America as a nation:

> You, you're the one.
> So loving, strong, and patient,
> Families like yours made all the states a nation.
> Our families are our past, our future and our pride.
> Whatever roots we come from, we're growing side by
>   side. (Quoted in Goldman, 1992, p. 93)

The song reflects the right-wing ideological notion that the family produced the character that permitted the development of democratic society. The inclusive pronouns— "you, you're, our"—connect McDonald's to "us." The ideology of the melting pot, signified by the line "Whatever roots we come from," is betrayed by the visual representation of a white middle-class family whenever the pronoun "yours" is sung. On the surface promoting the ethnically inclusive notion of the melting pot, the ad subtly hails "your" family and the true American family as white and middle-class. Thus, the racial politics of Golden Arches are mystified, given the appearance of tolerance but ideologically encoded in a contradictory and disturbing manner.

Promoting Conventional Morality and Sentimental Americana

As a part of its ideological world-making and garnering of public consent, McDonald's advertising also struggles to appropriate the meanings of cultural traditions and connect them to the Golden Arches. It is not trying to instigate instant hamburger sales with such ads: The strategy is much more complex. The point is to convince the public of the company's moral foundation and win the society's trust. "How could McDonald's sell us unhealthy food," hegemonized customers will ask, "when it is such a good company?" Scores of interviewees told me something like this, asserting that they are happy to take their children to McDonald's because the company does so much good—Ronald McDonald Houses, charities, sponsorship of athletic events, and more. Not only are McDonald's products validated, but the company itself, its right to economic and political power, and the political system that allows it to operate. When I presented such interviewees with more overtly political questions, almost invariably they supported a free market and a political economy based on unfettered free enterprise. They did not always express their political opinions self-consciously and with such labels, but their support for such precepts was obvious. For example, some interviewees contended, when asked about McDonald's social responsibility, "Corporations don't have social responsibilities." Yet others declared that corporations like McDonald's provide greater social benefits than any other social institution. One young man insisted:

> The best way for a person to help society is to make a lot of money—just like Ray Kroc did—and then use that money for good causes. Nobody does more to help the society than McDonald's with its children's charities, Ronald McDonald Houses, and support of athletics. Everybody else just talks about social responsibility; McDonald's has the money to make a real difference. I'd rather see corporations like McDonald's who have family values and believe in God helping people than the bureaucrats in the federal government. (Interview, 1998)

Thus, many McDonald's advertisements that celebrate conventionality and the status quo manage to appropriate their legitimating power. Instead of projecting itself as an engine of boring sameness and standardization, McDonald's spins itself as the rock of stability (read: moral stability) in a dangerous world of flux (Goldman and Papson, 1996; Kellner, 1992; Martin and Schumann, 1997). As a reporter for *Fortune* put it:

> Rather than being bored with McDonald's sameness, we learned to appreciate it. In a world where one of my ancestral homes became an on-ramp for the Illinois tollway and another was claimed for an atomic accelerator site, McDonald's became a symbol of stability. A McDonald's meal tastes pretty much the same everywhere. It can cure homesickness and makes strange places less strange. I brightened up considerably when after a long day on Guam earlier this year the golden arches greeted me around a bend. (Moser, 1994, p. 115)

"McDonald's, America, the family, private property, and you," ads have subliminally chanted over the last few decades. The consequences of the ideological victory of this signifying practice are all around us, with Ronald McDonald hailing us as statues of Lenin did in the former Soviet Union.

Lenins, however, were found mostly within the borders of the Soviet Union; Ronald and his Golden Arches call out to us almost everywhere, creating an ever more monotonous field of vision around the planet. And this field of vision is conjoined with a field of politics and morality that exerts an amazing ideological power, penetrating both the innermost individual consciousness and the largest expanses of geographic territory ever known.

Within its arsenal of cultural appropriations, McDonald's deploys a sentimental Americana, a syrupy patriotism that drapes the flag around the Golden Arches. John Caputo (1998) maintains that this Americana signifier has been used around the world to connect notions of hard work and leisure. Because of Americans' hard work, the story goes, they can afford nice things and they merit leisure—"you deserve a break today." In addition, Caputo argues, McDonald's Americana associates the company with and even makes it part of the American Dream—"a spouse, job, child, house, car, freedom, naturalness, informality, and self-sufficiency" (1998, p. 47). In many places in the world and, obviously, in the United States, absorbing such meanings makes McDonald's a powerful institution able to change people's views of themselves, their goals, their vision of success, and their understanding of their relationship to the world. What we have here is a semiotically charged cultural pedagogy, which, while providing power to McDonald's, shapes the way the world views the American nation-state. The way individuals receive this view of America varies—in some, a complex feeling of envy is combined with strong resentment.

In this context it is important to understand that throughout its history McDonald's advertising has represented the company not simply as an American institution, but as America itself. As the "land we love" writ small, McDonald's attaches itself to red, white, and blue patriotism at a variety of levels. Before the globalization process of the last two decades, Kroc understood that he was selling America not simply hamburgers but a vision of itself (Luxenberg, 1985). And, much to his entrepreneurial credit, Kroc's McDonald's captured the American imagination by connecting the restaurant to a lifestyle: specifically, that of the tanned, hip middle class from the late 1950s and early 1960s in the Los Angeles suburbs glorified by the Beach Boys in songs like "I Get Around." We're mobile, we're "real big wheels," and we're "making real good bread." Let's go surfing—on the way back we'll stop at McDonald's. From the All-American Marching Band and the All-American basketball and football teams to the All-American Meal served by All-American boys and girls, the All-American of the year, Ray Kroc, successfully connected the American signifier to McDonald's.

To display his support for American policy during the Vietnam War, Kroc announced that the American flag would fly 24 hours a day at McDonald's. Using the flag as the backdrop for the perpetually changing hamburger count, Kroc watched the burger numbers supplant the Dow Jones average as the symbolic statistical index for America's economic health. For Kroc the perpetually flying flag was a statement to anti-American war protesters and civil rights "kooks" that McDonald's/America would not stand for anyone criticizing or attempting to undermine our country (Kroc, 1977). There was no room for multiple meanings of the American signifier." In the 1960s no expenses were spared, no signifiers were left free-floating, in Kroc's effort to transfer reverence for America to McDonald's. The McDonald's outlet of the 1960s and 1970s was a shrine to

Americana and free enterprise, with obligatory plastic eagles. Banners in the bald eagles' beaks read, "McDonald's: The American Way" (Boas and Chain, 1976, p. 152).

Because the ideology of Americana works so well, Americans (and increasing numbers of the inhabitants of the world at large) do not talk much about power. When I asked people how McDonald's as a political power-wielder had shaped them, I was met with blank stares and hints of anger. On one level, I knew, it was a dumb ethnographic question, but I was as much interested in the emotional reaction to the question as in what anyone might have to say.

> *Interviewer (J. K.):* "What does it mean to argue that McDonald's power involves the ability to ascribe meanings to various features of our lives?"
>
> *Interviewee (white male in New York City):* "What the fuck are you talking about?" (1998)

The All-American ad campaigns of the sixties and seventies cost more money than any campaign in corporate advertising history. The purpose was to imbue the hamburger with a star-spangled signification. Americans, and ultimately people around the globe, began to make the desired connection.

As one of the ultimate icons of Americana, McDonald's (like Disney) transcends its status as a business establishment. When McDonald's or Disney speaks, it speaks for all of us. How could the Pirates of the Caribbean or (to stay with the pirate theme) Captain Crook of McDonaldland mislead us? The mere suggestion of such a possibility astonished many interviewees. Drawing upon similar signifiers and producing similar ideologies, McDonald's and Disney have climbed into bed together in recent years with cross-promotions. The ideological and historical connections between these bloody defenders of the status quo are fascinating. Politically aware Americans of the third decade of the nineteenth century saw mystical implications in the deaths of Thomas Jefferson and John Adams on July 4, 1826, the fiftieth anniversary of the Declaration of Independence. Culturally aware Americans of today may see similar implications in the fact that Ray Kroc and Walt Disney were in the same company in the U.S. Army. Both having lied about their age, the two prophets of free enterprise, conventional morality, and sentimental Americana fought the good fight for the American Way. Does it take anything away from the mystical connection to know that Kroc described Disney as a "strange duck" (Donald? Uncle Scrooge? Daisy?) because he wouldn't chase girls? (Kroc, 1977, p. 19). Whatever the answer, one thing is certain: Kroc and Disney have ideologically appropriated burgers and mice and taken them to places no previous burgers and mice have gone before.

Reflecting the Logic of Capital

In another facet of the McDonald's–Disney alliance, the two bastions of corporate morality have recently opened a factory in Vietnam where 17-year-old girls work 10 hours a day for six cents an hour producing Disney character toys to be given away with McDonald's Happy Meals. While earning their $4.20 per 70-hour week in February 1997, 200 young women at the plant fell ill, 25 collapsed, and three were taken to the hospital because of exposure to toxic chemicals (Emery, 1997). When I use the phrase "the ideology of the logic of capital," the McDonald–Disney factory in Vietnam provides a concrete example of the concept: In order to make huge profit margins on Happy Meal giveaways of Disney characters from, say, *101 Dalmatians*, the corporations employ young Vietnamese women in obscene working conditions. McDonald's operates, to put it simply, in line with a logic of capital that puts profits over the well-being of people.

This logic of capital is promoted by television, not simply in McDonald's commercials but on a variety of levels, including news programming, the content of dramas and comedies, and other advertising. The television medium is owned and operated by McDonald's corporate partners— Disney, for example, owns ABC outright—and this political-economic dynamic is constantly reflected in all phases of television programming. In the postmodern condition the logic of capital performs much of its work in the cultural domain, creating in the process a culture that is politically and economically charged beyond a level previously imaginable. This politicized and ideologized culture is far better equipped to channel and rechannel desire than the traditional political realm with its heavy-handed despotism. Thus, in the cultural realm of television and other forms of entertainment, the logic of capital facilitates McDonald's gaining new forms of power that are accountable to fewer and fewer people. As McDonald's power expands, it becomes one of a few giants participating in the global food industry. Millions of farmers around the world go out of business, while a few large companies, including McDonald's, gain a stranglehold on the production of food. In this context McDonald's deploys the ideology of the logic of capital to promote the idea that, because of the dangers of big government, the people are best served by the privatization of government functions—the creation of a corporate government (on privatization in general, cf. Best and Kellner, 1991; Kellner, 1990; Kovel, 1997; Vidal, 1997).

Thus, the ideology of capital works to justify corporate power. Because McDonald's and other transnational corporations have no boundaries and ignore national borders, they are unencumbered in their creation not simply of a corporate government, but a corporate *planetary* government. In this new arrangement McDonald's draws on the resources of public relations experts, market researchers, opinion pollsters, management consultants, computer industry executives, cable- and satellite-owners, other corporate entertainment managers (Disney, for example), and, of course, advertisers to create an unprecedented form of power—techno-power. In this process, capital gains a degree of power to justify itself, to shape the public's consciousness about both capital and themselves, that dwarfs previous efforts. In the world created by the justification of capital, McDonald's and other corporate executives can disseminate messages that influence the choices people make in amazingly subtle ways.

One of the best examples of this process involves the re-education of workers around the world—part of the larger right-wing re-education project referred to above. In order to increase profits McDonald's and other corporations must convince the public that the planet's economic health depends on lowering wages, decreasing social benefits, increasing worker hours per week, and refusing to improve working conditions. Since McDonald's is one of the biggest corporate employers in the world, its success in promoting this agenda, in hiding its alienated labor under the signifiers of conventional morality and Americana, plays an important ideological role in the globalized economy (on corporations in general, see Martin and Schumann, 1997).

Doug Kellner (1998) describes working at McDonald's as "an extremely blatant and degrading form of low-paid and alienated labor which is a career dead-end" (p. x). Prime examples of worker de-skilling, McJobs are so routinized that workers rarely have to make decisions. Rules have been designed for almost everything; if an unprecedented situation presents itself, workers are trained to consult a manager. Restaurants are "labor-proofed": Soft-drink dispensers are set to pour regular, medium, and large drinks automatically, and cash registers are programmed to allow a counter-waiter simply to press a button with a picture or the name of the product ordered. No calculations on the worker's part are necessary, as the cash registers total the costs, add tax, and tell the worker how much change to return to customers. If a customer orders a main meal without a dessert, the cash registers remind the worker to suggest a hot apple pie or an ice cream sundae. As far as cooking is concerned, most of McDonald's provisions arrive already cut, diced, sliced, molded, and fused by automated technologies. Workers basically reheat the products when needed and serve them to hungry McDonaphiles (Leidner, 1993; Ritzer, 1993, pp. 11, 105).

Looking to the "jobless future," McDonald's is working to replace more and more of these deskilled workers with robots. In many restaurants McRobots already prepare fries and pour drinks without human aid. When asked if robots will put many people out of work, McDonald's managers provide the perfect "ideology of capital" response. "Absolutely not," they insist. Instead of harming the interests of employees, the machine (named ARCH, for "automated restaurant crew helper") will provide "McDonald's employees with a tremendous opportunity to work with technology." And besides, executives confide, "The crew just loves it" (Lawren, 1993, p. 29). Such pronouncements are reminiscent of the scene in Michael Moore's film *Roger and Me* where employees of the Flint, Michigan, General Motors plant are induced to applaud as the last vehicle produced there rolls off the line. The workers are applauding their own unemployment. Portraying General Motors and McDonald's workers as loving their own dehumanization is a dramatic ideological moment. Within such moments, ideology succeeds in shaping human consciousness to accept the logic of capital as a natural aspect of the world. McDonald's campaign to represent its jobs as good and rewarding work is a case study in ideology management. A recent flyer (1997) put it this way:

GOOD JOBS FOR GOOD PEOPLE

Looking for a good job? Look no further than McDonald's.

If you're still in school, we can offer you the chance to learn valuable skills for your future while you earn extra spending money.

If you have young children and only want to work part time, we can give you flexible hours while you earn the extra income a growing family needs.

If you're retired and want a job that lets you meet people and have fun while you earn a little extra cash, McDonald's can give you that too.

If you think a job at McDonald's sounds like a good idea, don't wait. Fill out the attached application and talk to a member of our management team today.

Tomorrow, you could have a job.

Many print and television journalists concur that McDonald's workers enjoy their jobs. One of the secrets of McDonald's success, *Reader's Digest* contends, is that "newly hired employees are urged to have McFun" (Ola and d'Aulaire, 1988, p. 44). McDonald's management beseeches workers to "Join the Family." Promoting the logic of capital involves convincing workers and citizens in general that corporations like McDonald's always look out for the best interests of their workers.

Special ad campaigns praise workers and court their favor as part of a larger effort to keep them out of unions. Since here at McDonald's we have good workers, the ads tell us, we must respect them and consider them part of a family. Thus, McDonald's laborers will have no reason to consider organizing. Hidden in these ideological maneuvers is management's obsession with direct control over its workers. In reality, workers must gain managers' permission to go to the bathroom or get a drink; managers retain total control over working hours and can change employee hours anytime; and managers use the rationale of maintaining flexibility to justify limiting employee rights to those protected by the state (Vidal, 1997, pp. 221–22).

McDonald's managers and executives will not admit the existence of alienated and unhappy workers in the McFamily. No matter how many workers participate in anti-McDonald's labor organizations or self-organized groups, McManagers—like the early Bishop of Rome who refused to recognize the existence of a giraffe—deny their reality. Indeed, McDonald's management continues to devise training programs that indoctrinate workers and develop new surveillance procedures to monitor their compliance (Leidner, 1993, pp. 8–9; McSpotlight, 2001 [www.mcspotlight.org/issues/employment/index.html]; Ritzer, 1993, pp. 168–69). As long as people are desperate for work and corporate-friendly political conditions last, McDonald's, along with other fast food companies, will have no incentive to change ideological management strategies or working conditions. All fast food companies pay dismal wages. The only people who make less money than fast food workers are migrant farm workers (Schlosser, 1998a, 2001). Given its fidelity to the logic of capital and the resulting labor practices, McDonald's may not be as "huggable" as many seem to think.

3 McDonald's as a Postmodern Phenomenon

Not everyone agrees that contemporary sociopolitical, economic, and cultural life exhibits a new form of cultural logic. I maintain, however, that particular features of contemporary life are unique and distinct from what has come before—but they co-exist with previously existing modernist currents. The interaction of these unique postmodern features with extant modernist dynamics can easily be seen at McDonald's. In many ways the company provides a window on these complex cultural processes. In this chapter I focus on the corporation's often overlooked postmodern aspects.

The Importance of the Sign and Other Postmodern Features of the Golden Arches

In the postmodern context, individuals are rendered more vulnerable than ever to the power of the image. McDonald's and other corporate advertisers have exploited the power of the sign, but they are not the only ones. In politics the sign or signifier is dominant and all-pervasive. Understanding the tenuous nature of meaning in contemporary hyperreality, political media advisors recognize that their charge is to create comforting signs of common values for a melange of transient citizens who are unsure of what it all means. If successful, the political operatives will induce citizens to attach these semiotically rich images to their client (candidate). Often the rational content of the client's message is less important than the signifiers chosen by these handlers. Right-wing movements have taken advantage of this postmodern confusion and the increased power of the sign to connect signifiers of the European cultural heritage, the "true Americanness" of laissez-faire economics, knowledge of the traditional Western canon, and the values of a heterosexual nuclear family life to their organizations and political candidates. McDonald's has set the standard for such exploitation of the sign, making use of most of these right-wing signifiers to enhance its positive image with the public.

A Climate of Deceit

New media technologies expand power's use of knowledge to colonize individual consciousness and exacerbate a climate of deceit.

By engaging individuals at the level of emotion and affect and influencing the formation of their identities by the use of evocative signifiers, the messages of advertisers and politicos in hyperreality exert effects never before imagined. Indeed, in advertisements, political pronouncements, and much electronic entertainment, we find a postmodern culture of deceit. Just as the CIA has been known to produce disinformation designed to undermine "the enemy" and create conditions favorable to CIA interests, corporations and their advertisers often distribute data that create a facade of understanding while actually moving people to a new level of confusion. In Chapter 1 I describe this dynamic as a expression of "cultural pedagogy"—a form of out-of-school teaching that provides people with their most important information, shapes their identities, and helps form their values. In a climate of deceit, such a process works in the interests of the producer of information, not the receiver. An informational politics of deceit demands a public awareness campaign to alert citizens to the power of signs and their influence on our ways of seeing the world.

McDonald's presents an exemplary case. Its advertising to children on the value of its food emphasizes dietary balance, variety, and good nutrition. The assistant attorney general of Texas, Stephen Gardner, as well as officials from New York State and California, responded in 1985 that the food could not be deemed nutritious; they threatened to charge McDonald's with false advertising (*Consumer Reports*, 1988, pp. 356–57).

In a 1997 interview Gardner spoke of his work with McDonald's in Texas:

> We learned that McDonald's was advertising its products as basically nutritious and healthy [and] from our examination of the . . . nutritional information, in our opinion the foods generally contained so much sodium and fat and so [few] helpful ingredients that they just flat weren't nutritious. Because of that we wrote to McDonald's and told them to stop. Stop using these advertisements, stop claiming that McDonald's food was nutritious. (McSpotlight, 1997)

After numerous letters were exchanged between McDonald's and the Texas attorney general's office,

> the ads were pulled[.] McDonald's claims, as I understand it, was that [it] was just a natural happenstance. My experience is, and I've dealt with a lot of companies doing falsely deceptive advertising and ironically it seems that they always made the decision to stop running the ads the moment before my

letter got there telling them that the ads were deceptive, so, it's an exercise in guesswork that I don't care to engage in as to whether or not our letters stopped them. I do know, and I do believe at any rate that our letters prevented them from doing things additionally in the future in this area. (Ibid.)

The British Advertising Standards Authority forced McDonald's to withdraw two newspaper ads in 1990 and 1991 (McSpotlight, 1997). One claimed falsely that the company used fewer food additives than it actually did; the other asserted misleading claims concerning the recyclability of its packaging. Numerous consumer protection agencies (such as the National Food Alliance in Great Britain) decided that the company's record of deceit made it absurd to entrust the monitoring of McDonald's advertising to industry associations (McSpotlight, 1997). As far as consumer groups are concerned, McDonald's advertising budget and media presence make it a major producer of knowledge, an important molder of public consciousness, and a master deceiver. After some misleading statements by McDonald's concerning the use of beef fat in frying, *Consumer Reports* described how the company operates when charged with duplicitous behavior:

> McDonald's then managed to turn the bad press into a marketing opportunity—"to neutralize the junk-food misconceptions about McDonald's good food," the company told its operators. It launched a multimillion-dollar advertising campaign stressing dietary "balance" and "variety" while extolling the good nutrition customers can glean at the Golden Arches—like calcium from calcium-enriched buns. The ads were so one-sidedly positive about the nutritional possibilities at McDonald's that the company was asked to cease and desist. (1988, p. 357)

Depoliticization Via Social Vertigo

The knowledge explosion saturates the landscape with information, resulting in the fragmentation of meaning, a social vertigo, and a social amnesia. The whole process promotes depoliticization—the lack of concern with and knowledge of power and justice.

Analysts of contemporary society observe a changing world, a hyperreality marked by a social vertigo. The situation is in many ways analogous to the modernist industrial changes John Dewey documented at the beginning of the twentieth century. When Dewey (1916) called for novel ways of thinking and fresh modes of analysis to better understand the emerging aspects of the society, he did not argue that there was no continuity between mid-nineteenth-century America and the world emerging in the early twentieth century. His focus, understandably, was on the unprecedented, as he attempted to convince the public of the need to address the challenges to democracy presented by new problems. My analysis is similar to Dewey's. At the beginning of the twenty-first century, constructions of time and cultural space are changing in relation to the electronic images bombarding us from local, national, and international venues. Social dislocations result. Given the informational focus of many of these changes, meaning is fragmented. With so much information bombarding their senses, many lose faith that they can make sense of anything. The social vertigo that results attracts the attention of critical analysts, who explore the process of its production, focusing on the relationship between information technology and power.

As industrialization and technology have evolved, power has become increasingly difficult to identify. Perpetually disguised, power has exerted its influences so subtly that most are unaware of the oppression at work in their lives. Many who are aware are induced to do nothing about it. Those who produce information must seduce the consumptive public into collaboration. The production and dispersion of seductive images requires financial resources available only to extremely large firms and industries. As the pace of transmission, reception, and production speeds up, the values of the instant and the throwaway penetrate all dimensions of contemporary life—fast food is tailor-made for fast capitalism in an accelerated postmodern society. Such instantaneity and disposability extend beyond fast food and McDonald's, as values, lifestyles, and relationships become obsolescent. As meaning is destabilized, as more happens in a given period of time, individuals begin to lose touch with what came before the instant. Time dislocation undermines our personal and social histories, in the process decontextualizing our identities and institutions. This atrophy of memory or social amnesia has profound consequences, for as the past is forgotten, its power over the present is obscured. The amnesia makes "what is" seem as if "it had to be."

When erasure-of-memory is succeeded by informational campaigns designed to create new memories, social vertigo is exacerbated. Many are familiar with the Dean Witter ads where a grainy, "antiqued" film quality is used to convey the impression that we are watching a historical depiction of the firm's origin myth: a bespectacled 1930s-esque "Dean Witter" telling his staff of their sacred obligation to the individual needs of the customer. Many people I have interviewed are shocked to discover that these ads are not authentic. A recent (1990) McDonald's ad campaign also creates memory by presenting a nostalgic, sentimentalized, and conflict-free American family pictorial history. The ads create a true-blue American historical role for McDonald's where there was none before. You can almost hear in your imagination the male voice-over: "Though we didn't yet exist, we were there to do it all for you—McDonald's then, McDonald's now."

As hyperreality produces such pseudo-memories, our ability to find meaning, to engender the passion necessary for commitment, is undermined. Americans are increasingly oblivious to politics, even as they have become increasingly sensitive to culture—popular culture in particular. Most twenty-first-century Americans ignore questions of power, justice, income distribution, and control of information. The attempt to raise such issues in hyperreality is greeted with boredom and even anger (Grossberg, 1992, 306–7). My effort on the radio to speak of McDonald's as a political phenomenon was viewed as absurd and, interestingly, tasteless. One of my interviewees responded to a question on the political implications of McDonald's:

> McDonald's political implications? I don't see anything political about McDonald's or their advertisements. What do hamburgers have to do with elections? Are you saying that people who eat McDonald's food will vote for certain candidates? If that's what you're saying then I don't agree. That's silly. People are not going to vote for who McDonald's or anybody else tells them to. Is McDonald's saying we should vote for a particular person? I never heard that. (Interview, 1998)

In the contemporary United States, most people, like this interviewee, equate politics with "electoral politics," not with issues of power and its distribution. Given this interviewee's construction of the meaning of "power," I could empathize with her confusion. When I clarified the question and explained that I was thinking not so much about electoral politics as about power and its distribution, she was still confused about the meaning of the term "political."

The power of elites or postmodern information-producers is tolerable only if it is well masked. Corporate power-wielders in contemporary society are so adept at cloaking their influence that an increasingly depoliticized population gives them carte blanche to shape the world. Television, which was supposed to increase citizen knowledge and political participation, has been so manipulated by power-wielders that it has actually decreased people's desire to participate in the political realm. Many argue that the corporate control of the medium has contributed to the production of a privatized, consumer society at the expense of civic interest. News programs provide detailed coverage of mainstream figures while neglecting the ideas of groups and individuals critical of existing cultural arrangements. Advertisements construct a world where commodity consumption solves social and political problems—the stress of contemporary life, signified by "you deserve a break today," can be eased by a Big Mac and fries. The corporate advertisement's "we" induces consumers to align their interests and identities with the impersonal power-wielders—interests that would include political support to help "us" create a good business climate through lower corporate taxes and state, local, and national incentives to locate in "our" communities. When McDonald's promotes the signifier "My McDonald's," we are seduced into joining the corporate sign community that is everywhere but nowhere. Although highly political, the sign community is represented in a manner that removes it from the political domain. It may be where we find personal and familial pleasure, but it has nothing to do with the political. The political is represented as that unpleasant realm where elections take place and unseemly deals are made (Airakinsen, 1992; Kellner, 1990, p. 174).

Over the last few decades corporations have successfully undermined society's understanding of the political. Terms such as "ideological," "domination," and "hegemonic" are not known, nor do they seem appropriate in contemporary society. The corporate ads tell us that there are two realms in the world: the cultural and the material (the political-economic). Never will the realms intersect with one another, for one's likes and dislikes in relation to commodities have nothing to do with the political world.

Marc Cooper (1998) provides an excellent example of depoliticization at work in contemporary free-marketeered, corporatized Chile. Having worked in Chile in the early seventies during the Salvador Allende regime, Cooper was fascinated by that society's political passion around issues of social justice and the public good. Returning to the corporatized Chile of 1998, Cooper painfully documented the expanding influence of McDonald's and other national and international corporations and the corresponding change in public consciousness. Cooper writes of a social amnesia, an embrace of free market values, an obsession with social mobility and bourgeois status at all costs, and a breakdown of community solidarity in favor of privatized citizenship. The once politically well-informed Chilean society is not even a distant memory, as citizens operate in the allegedly nonpolitical realm of consumer capitalism. It may be easier for North Americans to recognize these sociopolitical dynamics when they occur outside national boundaries.

Cynicism and Hypermotivation

The fragmentation of meaning produces both a new form of cynicism that destroys faith in social narratives and the phenomenon of hypermotivation.

Cynicism has reached crisis levels at the beginning of the twenty-first century. As the postmodern icon David Letterman insinuates with his hip humor: "I may be stupid and uninformed, but at least I'm not going to be duped by some phony TV or advertising promotion. My fans and I know what you (power-wielders) are up to. We don't believe we can do anything about it, but we're not your dupes."

This cynicism is easy to understand in a context where companies bolster their sign value by exploiting beliefs and emotional investments. Typically advertisers use such signifiers until they squeeze much of the meaning out of them. For example, McDonald's and other companies have used family values and the love between family members to the point that promotions of this kind have lost some of their emotional impact. When such a loss is perceived, McDonald's drops these campaigns and waits until the family signifiers regain some of their meaning. Yet the process has long-lasting effects: When family love is used to sell Big Macs, some of its sanctity slips away and cynicism grows.

Cynicism undermines belief structures without providing alternative ways of making meaning. People are often left with little to believe in. As a result, bizarre ways of seeing arise, from zealous fundamentalist religious sects and racial hate groups to occultism—and attract people with nothing left to lose. The corporate world has given birth to a cultural phenomenon that, for want of a better word, might be called hypermotivation. People who are hypermotivated exhibit a nervous restlessness and a narrow focus on the world. Examples might include workaholic corporate men and women obsessed with careerist and consumerist goals. Even better representatives, perhaps, are the true-believing Amway salespeople, since the Amway image implies a wild enthusiasm for nothing in particular save enthusiasm itself (Lash, 1990). Give me something—anything—to believe in, to be passionate about. McDonald's executives often fit into this pattern as they search for manager-trainees who are willing to become hypermotivated about membership in the

McFamily. High-fee motivational consultants travel from business to business, staff meeting to staff meeting: "When I give the signal," they tell their hypermotivatees, "stand and cheer yourselves! Motivate yourselves, you can do it, today is the first day of the rest of your lives." They save souls, winning converts for hypermotivated free enterprise. When meaning is lost, then affect becomes its own reward—a revival without a cause.

The "McDonald's vision," as it is labeled, is postmodern hypermotivation *par excellence*. "To what do you attribute your success?" McDonald's executives are repeatedly asked. "The McDonald's vision," they answer (Salva-Ramirez, 1995–96, p. 30). Such responses are often followed by awkward silences because no one is quite sure what the vision involves. Could it be the resurrection of Ray Kroc? The transubstantiation of burger into flesh? The vision is not clear at this point, but whatever it might be, it is inculcated into franchisees, managers, and assistant managers at Hamburger University. McDonald's literature reports that after graduation each "hamburgerologist," as they are called, carries the hypermotivated torch, "the brand and breed of corporate loyalty," "the esprit de corps" of the Golden Arches (ibid., p. 31). With four Hamburger Universities around the world—in the United States, Germany, Britain, and Japan—McDonald's is hypermotivating the planet with its nebulous vision (ibid.).

Back at their home outlets the hamburgerologists fan the jihad of hypermotivation with employee rallies, where, according to one report, employees "literally rock from the chandeliers." The chandelier rocking, one hamburgerologist said, "tells us we've hit the mark, that we've shown people there's a heck of an opportunity here, that we're an organization that really cares, and an employer they can be proud of" (Flynn, 1996, p. 55). Really cares for what? Be proud of what? The vision of what? Believe the hype, the hamburgerologists tell their folds. Don't question, just feel the power. Are we feeling cynical yet?

Discomfort with the Profound

As knowledge producers and other individuals become increasingly uncomfortable with the profound, surface meanings are celebrated.

Part of the postmodern condition is a tendency to focus on the surface, on "the look," the image. Peter McLaren (1991) and Stanley Aronowitz (1983) describe the "literalness of the visual"—a phenomenon whereby individuals have trouble seeing beneath the surface of visual or media images. As a result the concepts explored here in relation to McDonald's such as power, identity, globalization, and context—none of which are instantly accessible to the senses—are erased from public awareness. In the 1980s this tendency was well represented by Ronald Reagan's superficial explanations of complex political processes; in the first decade of the twenty-first century, George W. Bush deftly carries the torch of superficiality. In the context of the Golden Arches, we can see the process at work on a variety of levels. No aspect is more disconcerting than the profound shallowness of the "McDonald's type" of man (he has traditionally been male) whom personnel managers are seeking.

Ray Kroc vehemently rejected educated people as McDonald's employees. If we analyze Kroc's hiring philosophy and many of the individuals with whom he surrounded himself, it is clear that the King of the Burger sought out one-dimensional men with a Mickey Spillane twist. Described by some analysts as "quirky, iconoclastic, and downright bizarre" (Ellis, 1986, p. 19; cf. Love, 1986), they were also

consistently shallow, ill-informed, and content not to question the surface meanings of what they encountered. John
Love reveals that Engineering Chief James Schindler, a member of Kroc's inner circle, spent hours arguing "that man's
perfection approaches only 64 percent of God's" (1986, p.
104). Indeed, the hamburgerologists are prototypes for postmodern men of little substance, purveyors of a theology of
shallowness (Ellis, 1986). Such hirings have produced institutional problems that continue to plague McDonald's. Much
of the internal fighting that marked life at corporate headquarters in the 1990s involved what the company should do
about this tradition of shallowness (Machan, 1998).

Kroc seemed unperturbed by meetings of high-level
managers where corporate leaders spent hours arguing
about the degree to which man could achieve perfection.
Lacking a high school diploma himself, Kroc seemed determined to prove that McDonald's did not need "deep
thinkers," as he called them (Ellis, 1986, p. 19). Often urg-
ing young people to leave school and go to work, Kroc proclaimed: "There are too many baccalaureates and not
enough butchers" (Vidal, 1997, p. 25). As McDonald's men
we have "ketchup in our veins," executives tell reporters
(Solomon, 1996, p. 50). The term the company uses to signify this postmodern shallowness is "corporate values." They
are not interested in restaurateurs but in individuals with an
"entrepreneurial flair" who adopt McDonald's corporate values (Salva-Ramirez, 1995–96, p. 30). Such workers keep
their noses clean, look straight ahead, and do not question
the avalanche of corporate rules all McDonald's managers
and executives must follow. Individuals without corporate
values might think too much about the logic of their hypermotivation, causing a crisis of purpose, an unwelcome exis-
tential moment of reflection.

In the globalized culture of McDonald's, these corporate values are often translated as "American values." Upon entering a new country, the company's personnel head-hunters seek out "foreigners" with ketchup in their veins, "skills that complement their corporate values" (*Personnel Journal*, 1994, p. 12). In personality profiles in business publications, McDonald's managerial stars frequently stress their "corporate values," often connecting themselves to All-Americanism and Dale Carnegie–type positive thinking. One McDonald's field consultant in Boston was characterized by a reporter for *Forbes* (Machan, 1988) as: (1) being as American as a Big Mac; (2) loving the Olympics; (3) having played college football; (4) always wearing his seat belt; (5) saying the words "correctomundo" and "outstanding" all the time because he is a positive guy; and (6) loving his wife and kids but cherishing, most of all, his job at McDonald's. These Dale Carnegies of grease have learned many of the positive-thinking rituals: Always smile, look people directly in the eye, and talk and ask questions about topics in which the person you are with is interested. What happens when McCarnegies run into one another? What do they talk about? Maybe Hamburger University offers a seminar on avoiding the pitfalls of such an encounter.

Profiles in the business press suggest that Den Fujita, chief operating officer of McDonald's Japan, is the embodiment of the corporation's postmodern shallowness. Looking for a CEO to run its Japanese operation, McDonald's managers sifted through scores of applicants with impressive business credentials involving the administration of major enterprises and then, following its typical modus operandi, passed them over in favor of Fujita. The eccentric Fujita had the right stuff for McDonald's management. He argued that as a fish-eating people the Japanese are "pale-faced and undignified." They need to eat red meat, Fujita concluded (Katayama, 1986, p. 116). After taking the reins in Japan, Fujita began to issue freakish racial theories concerning the commercial acumen of businessmen from Osaka, including himself. (Individuals familiar with company history may have recalled the speech about lazy operators delivered at the corporation's First International Conference—see Chapter 2.) Fujita theorized that a group of Jews—who, he maintained, like all Jews, had natural business talent—settled in Osaka in some lost period of history. His one shred of evidence is the fact that Osaka's official symbol looks vaguely like the Star of David. Actually, it is a maritime channel marker that some say resembles a three-stemmed wineglass (Katayama, 1986). To publicize his theories Fujita wrote *The Jewish Way of Doing Business*, a work marked by disconcerting generalizations about the Jewish people and their business practices (ibid., p. 116).

Michael Quinlan—CEO of the McDonald's Corporation from 1982 to 1998 and now chair of the company—is an enigma wrapped in a Happy Meal as he operates in the corporate culture's celebration of shallowness. If Quinlan had been more unusual, in the Kroc and Fujita manner, he might have been more secure in his position as CEO. But Quinlan is a Filet-O-Fish out of water at McDonald's. Not only does he pay insufficient homage to Kroc and his eccentricities (Deveny, 1988), but Quinlan has a bachelor's degree in psychology and philosophy and a night-school MBA from Loyola of Chicago. Observers often speak of Quinlan's sharp intellect. One former vice-chairman of the corporation tells of administering an aptitude test to a group of McDonald's executives. Quinlan easily scored the highest grade on the exam, but, as even the corporate-booster *Business Week* pointed out, the competition was not especially tough (ibid.). As McDonald's ran into stiffer domestic competition and changing American tastes in the mid- and late 1990s, the early-rising, hard-working, no-nonsense Quinlan faced mounting criticisms and negative comparisons with his flamboyant corporate McAncestors (Horovitz, 1998a). In August 1998, Quinlan was demoted to chair and replaced by a new CEO, Jack Greenberg, who has even better educational credentials. Quinlan is simply not vacuous enough. He does not fit the mold of postmodern shallowness, and the McDonald's people confide to reporters that "he just doesn't have the right personality" (Horovitz, 1998a, p. 8B). It will be interesting to see how Greenberg fares in this bizarre corporate culture.

The Culture of Spectacle

Fascination replaces meaning as the spectacle becomes more important in all facets of everyday life.

A Diet Coke ad of the 1990s extends our understanding of contemporary society and McDonald's reflection of and influence on it: "Some people live their life as an exclamation not an explanation." The ad represents a powerful philosophical, even epistemological, revolution. What good does the philosopher's traditional need to explain the world do? it asks. To hell with reason, with analysis; as Diet Coke puts it: "You get to taste it all." There is no need for reflection here. Why think about the social, cultural, political, economic, ecological, nutritional, and moral aspects of food and eating when "McDonald's does it all for you"? Eating is a source of fascination and feeling, not something to ponder and connect to the complex process of food production and consumption. McDonald's removes food from the context of cooking and presentation, as it focuses consumers' attention on the "McDonald's experience." Removing consumers from their everyday routines, it makes food a dramatic spectacle, complete with Ronald McDonald, the McDonaldland characters, and indoor and outdoor playgrounds. Geared especially to children, the McDonald's spectacle suggests the larger postmodern obsession with entertainment, with the colonization of desire/libidinal energy as the most effective pathway to economic and political power. Not a new concept, for sure, but one that, when combined with electronic communication technologies, penetrates the most geographically distant reaches of the globe and the most private mind spaces of the individual.

The use of entertainment as the pathway to power has reshaped the cultural and political landscape of the contemporary era. A political figure may lie, cheat, and steal and still survive as long as he (typically not a she) is entertaining. In many ways food is similar. Many nutritionists and pediatricians maintain that portraying food as entertainment, as McDonald's commercials aimed at children do, substitutes amusement for nourishment and poses a health risk (McSpotlight, 1997).

This focus of American corporations on entertainment is central to understanding America's (Pyrrhic) victory in the Cold War. Ronald McDonald—not Nikita Khrushchev or Ronald Reagan—came out on top in the Texas Death Match of grand ideologies. Ronald's reign may be a short one because the ability to entertain cannot divert people's attention from unhealthy food and minimum-wage McJobs forever. Nevertheless, in the short run the leaders of America's globalized entertainment (broadly defined) industry boast of its ability to meet the needs of people around the globe because of the unfettered creative freedom of the American system. McDonald's, Disney, and Nike, it is argued, provide the world with a freedom that cannot be found anywhere else (Martin and Schumann, 1997). The needs McDonald's meets involve emotions and desires that are sold as *spectacle Americana*. McDonald's marketing connects the "eating experience" with "life as an exclamation," which is semiotically packaged to the world as a high-affect taste of American freedom. I'll have the WWF burger with the XFL fries.

McDonald's restaurants have always been physically constructed with spectacle in mind. The food preparation area is open to public view so that consumers can watch clean-cut employees in loud uniforms hustle around the shiny, stainless steel, institutional kitchen appliances. Hamburgers come in containers wrapped like a Christmas toy, connecting the unwrapping process to the happy signifier of holiday gifts. French fries are heavily exposed in shallow containers to create the impression of abundance—a cornucopia of goodies spilling over for your enjoyment. No wonder McDonald's and Disney climb into bed together for one co-marketing deal after another; both depend on their ability to conjure Hollywood magic. Kids learn the message quickly: Home cooking is not entertaining; McDonald's is.

The Chinese learned these lessons immediately after the first McDonald's opened near Tiananmen Square in Beijing in April 1992. Serving tens of thousands of customers a day with its 700 seats and 29 cash registers, the outlet quickly became a tourist attraction for the Chinese people. Seeking to build near tourist attractions around the world, McDonald's promotes a carnival ambiance with prizes and contests that is especially exotic to Chinese and non-American eyes. Understanding the importance of the spectacle, McDonald's ad agencies for the last three decades have emphasized the experience, not the food (Boas and Chain, 1976).

One much praised and rewarded McDonald's franchisee well understood the spectacular nature of the McDonald's experience. In quick succession he set up a series of promotions including: a deal with a local radio station at 1470 on the AM dial that everyone who came to his store 14 minutes and 70 seconds after several on-the-air announcements would receive a free hamburger; a raffle of a BMW in his outlet's parking lot; a contest to predict how long it would take 20 tons of ice to melt in the parking lot; and a rocking horse marathon, conceived after he found 30 abandoned rocking horses—a new car was awarded to the last person to leave (Luxenberg, 1985). Indeed, it is not simply about food—the little (and big) dramas keep bringing 'em in. When the Quarter Pounder was introduced in Honolulu, the company devised a Broadway song and dance routine featuring new kitchen machinery and hamburger patty characters (Boas and Chain, 1976).

And Kroc loved it; he reveled in the spectacle and the spotlight. His intense need for public acceptance and recognition made him the perfect promoter of McDonald's eating as spectacle. One can feel the ego gratification in Kroc's authorial voice as he describes a presentation at a home game played by the San Diego Padres, the team he owned: "The mayor presented me with an award. . . . the sportswriters also gave me an award, the U.S. Navy Band and Marine Band played, and cameras flashed as I stood there, arms raised, making the V-sign, acknowledging the cheers like a presidential candidate" (Kroc, 1977, p. 184). Not only was Kroc's McDonald's a spectacle, but Kroc himself had become an icon in the spectacular postmodern "cult of celebrity."

The more one knows about Kroc, the more fascinating and culturally significant he becomes. The importance of a showman in the food-as-entertainment business in the age of the spectacle is highlighted by Kroc's death on January 14, 1984 (Toy Zone, 1999). None of his successors—Fred Turner, Michael Quinlan, Jack Greenberg—has possessed Kroc's ability to embody the postmodern substitution of fascination for meaning. Like his friend Ronald Reagan, Kroc had a flair for colorful oversimplifications that played well in the era of the media sound bite, a time of superficiality and a loss of meaning (Boas and Chain, 1976, p. 160; Horovitz, 1998a, p. 8B; Love, 1995, p. 44). Kroc ran McDonald's like a family-values striptease, creating a loyal following that persists long after his death. Few entrepreneurs find themselves posthumously glorified in newspapers around the country for their style. A June 1997 headline in the *New York Times*, for example, asked in bold print: "Where Have You Gone, Ray Kroc?" (Feder, 1997). The Joe DiMaggio of hamburgers, the Reagan of fast food, Kroc left his mark on the way business is conducted in the Age of Spectacle. Kroc wannabe Dave Thomas of Wendy's attempted to emulate the master but settled for commodifying the fact that he was truly a boring guy. Mike Quinlan and Jack Greenberg, perpetually operating in Kroc's shadow, struggle to make McDonald's—not Mike Quinlan and Jack Greenberg—the story. Of course, this is the antithesis of the Kroc formula. Koo Kooka Jube, Mrs. Robinson, raucous Ray has left and gone away.

Fast Capitalism

Technocapitalism, or fast capitalism, based on neo-classical market values, operates to create a globalized economic order—a neo–Social Darwinism (Alfino, 1998; Best and Kellner, 1991; Goldman and Papson, 1996; Ritzer, 1993).

Changes in corporate behavior and business operations in the late twentieth and the early twenty-first centuries are a study in contrast and continuity—a reflection of the interaction of the modern and postmodern. Even though new technologies, modes of knowledge production, and sign systems have developed, the contemporary free enterprise system still reflects particular characteristics of its nineteenth-century take-off phase:

1. It is growth-oriented. Only growth can guarantee profits. Under this growth imperative, managers seek to achieve expansion regardless of the human, social, geopolitical, or ecological consequences. McDonald's, business writers often note, is a company consumed by the imperative to expand (Love, 1995, pp. 113–14; Luxenberg, 1985, p. 8).

2. Growth has traditionally required the exploitation of workers. This does not mean that labor gets nothing; it means that growth is based on the difference between what workers create and what they get. McDonald's low wages and deskilling practices are so notorious that the term "McJob" has come to signify degrading work in the service economy (Vidal, 1997, p. 215). (McDonald's itself uses the term as the name of a jobs program for the mentally and physically handicapped: see McSpotlight, 1997).

3. The free enterprise system places great emphasis on technological and organizational innovation. Competition demands that entrepreneurs constantly search for an edge over their business rivals (Harvey, 1989). McDonald's again has lent its name to innovative organizational practices: George Ritzer's concept of McDonaldization (Ritzer, 1993). As the corporation that many economists describe as ready to run over its competitors with a bulldozer, McDonald's is the paragon of the contemporary

multinational corporation (Kovel, 1997, pp. 30–31, quotes a *Wall Street Journal* headline stating that McDonald's "wants to run over its competition with a Mack truck").

The changes in capital accumulation have resulted in a savage new economic order that has changed and is continuing to change Western culture. Technocapitalism, as Doug Kellner (1989) describes it, becomes increasingly multinational as technologies like satellite television and computers carry forms of mass consumer culture throughout the world, colonizing previously private spaces. Making use of these technologies, technocapitalism moves money, ideas, information, images, technologies, and goods and services quickly from one country to another. If the "business climate" is not good enough in one place, a corporation will move, or at least threaten to move, to a more profitable venue. Such threats can undercut a locale's attempt to levy a corporate tax or workers' attempt to gain benefits or improve their wages. The twenty-first-century corporate culture of power is created by this financial Blitzkrieg.

As previously observed, technocapitalism uses consumer goods, film, television, mass images, and computerized information to shape desires and consciousness throughout both the developed and the developing world. In the context of a book about McDonald's, it is important to note that multinational technocapitalism is helping to shape a worldwide cultural change that dramatically enhances the power of those connected to the administration of these nomadic corporations. Individuals find it increasingly difficult to identify the reality of this growing power. It is administered less with an iron hand than with a velvet glove. Perpetually disguised, postmodern power has extended its influence so subtly that most people are unaware of the insidious oppression at work in their own lives.

In my interviews on McDonald's, I asked several people with college degrees to speak about what it might mean for a corporation to hold political power. In almost every case the interviewees speculated that such power would help the corporation get particular candidates elected. When asked to provide another example of how such power could be used, none of the respondents could think of one. This public unfamiliarity with the workings of power allows corporations and their right-wing supporters to enjoy dominance in the contemporary era. In this bizarre postmodern condition, technocapitalists have realized that power requires co-production by those who generate information and those who consume it. In this situation those who produce information must seduce various consumptive publics into collaboration (Luke, 1991).

In the process of exercising its new power over information and images, technocapitalism teaches a plethora of social and political lessons. Those who "make it" in the new globalized culture are those who operate on the basis of their self-interest. The concept of a larger social good—as opposed to a cynical corporate representation of social concern generated for image-building—begins to fade from the public radar screen. The seductive commodified images of individual choice, privatized lifestyles, and commercial interests share little space with collective needs.

Even when corporations address the social good, what emerges can be quite misleading. McDonald's, for example, represents itself as concerned with the environment, publicizing its alleged status as the world's biggest recycler of waste. What is not mentioned is that the company produces more trash than any other organization in the world

(Manning and Cullum-Swan, 1994, p. 265). McDonald's pamphlets and school materials stress the nutritional value of its food, omitting warnings from the medical community concerning its dangerously high levels of fat and calories (Manning and Cullum-Swan, 1994). The company presents itself as a model employer with happy and contented workers. Erased, of course, are statistics on pay, turnover, and union busting activity (Deetz, 1993).

The culture of McDonald's and the personality of Kroc meld. McDonald's as the theatrically disguised representative of a new globalized incarnation of a savage capitalism has taken its cues from the corporate culture Kroc established in the 1950s and 1960s. In fast capitalism we see the re-emergence of a corporate machismo, a neo-patriarchy exposed and in the interpretive eyes of many glorified by such movies as *Wall Street*, *Boiler Room*, and *Glengarry, Glenross*. Kroc was ahead of the game; for the first 10 years of its existence, the company under Kroc's direction refused to hire women at any level, even as secretaries. In Kroc's words:

> Clark told me I should hire a secretary.
> "I suppose you're right," I said, "But I want a male secretary. . . . I want a man. He might cost a little more at first, but if he's any good at all, I'll have him doing sales work in addition to administrative things. I have nothing against having a pretty girl around, but the job I have in mind would be much better handled by a man.". . . My decision to hire a male secretary paid off when I was hospitalized for a gall bladder operation and later for a goiter operation. [The male secretary] worked between our office and my hospital room, and we kept things humming as briskly as when I was in the office every morning. (Kroc, 1977, pp. 48–49)

Kroc once exclaimed that if McDonald's ever hired women to work at the restaurants, he wanted them to "be kind of flat-chested" so they wouldn't attract boys who would hang around and cause trouble (quoted in Ellis, 1986, p. 19). The one exception to Kroc's gender-exclusion policy in the early days was June Martino. Those who knew her regarded Martino as a gifted businesswoman whose expertise often kept the company going during difficult times. But Kroc's macho culture placed her in a different position from males on the staff. Kroc's own words about her are quite revealing:

> I thought it was good to have a lucky person around, maybe some of it would rub off on me. Maybe it did. After we got McDonald's going and built a larger staff, they called her "Mother Martino." She kept track of everyone's family fortunes, whose wife was having a baby, who was having marital difficulties, or whose birthday it was. She helped make the office a happy place. (Kroc, 1977, p. 84)

Kroc's attitudes came to permeate all levels of McDonald's organizational culture. Management was strikingly insensitive to gender issues such as sexual harassment well into the 1980s. My interviews with women managers revealed incidents in which 18- and 19-year-old women employees were pressured to go out with older male managers (interviews, 1994). My interviewees told me that the company suppressed reports of sexual harassment; women who complained were sometimes punished or forced to resign. One successful manager confided that after she reported harassment, company higher-ups stalked her both on and off the job. She was eventually forced to leave the company (interview, 1994). McDonald's gender politics was reflected in Kroc's personal life. During a party in the late 1960s thrown for him and his second wife, Jane, Kroc announced to virtually everyone's surprise that he was divorcing Jane to marry the wife of a McDonald's franchise-owner. Kroc seemed unembarrassed by such personal episodes (Love, 1995, p.

271). Indeed, his public pronouncements and writings communicate a social, cultural, and psychological unguardedness, a naiveté, that allows observers to peer deep into the forces that shaped him and his company—and, for that matter, contemporary American culture.

In these highly personal portraits, Kroc reveals a passion for organizational standardization; an inability to understand "others," be they African Americans, Latinos, or women; an insensitivity to what those who were culturally or racially different from him would find offensive; a lifelong hunger to be accepted by those with high social status; and an obsessive devotion to the defense of a radical free enterprise community. All of these revelations offer a deeper insight into the attitudes that have precipitated the rise of a neo–Social Darwinist political economy. When one follows the story of Kroc's interactions with Dick and Mac McDonald, who opened the first McDonald's in San Bernardino, California, in the 1940s, a disturbing picture emerges. Kroc wanted to buy the entire McDonald's operation, but Dick and Mac wanted to keep their San Bernardino store. They enjoyed owning the store and wanted to reward two of their long-term employees by letting them manage it. Kroc was infuriated. "What a goddam rotten trick," Kroc wrote in his autobiography, *Grinding It Out* (1977, p. 123). Bent on revenge, Kroc opened a McDonald's across the street from the original store and ran the brothers out of business—not an uncommon strategy for McDonald's, which has targeted local firms for decimation throughout the world (Luxenberg, 1985, pp. 8–9). The media gush about the all-American McDonald's success story rarely finds room for the stories of these thousands of displaced independent small-business owners.

In an era of savage capitalism, a company must operate in an especially brutal manner to merit a headline like the

Wall Street Journal's assertion that McDonald's "wants to run over its competition with a Mack Truck" (quoted in Kovel, 1997, p. 31). The proclamations of McDonald's aggressiveness are legendary; even the business journal *The Economist* labels the company's fixation with domination as verging on the "fanatical" (1996, p. 61). The cultural scholars David Bell and Gill Valentine contend that something in this business is "rotten at the core" (1997, p. 135). Yet McDonald's is powerful enough to control information about itself and deploy signifiers in a way that creates a public image of family values, child-friendliness, and civic responsibility.

Jeff Weinstein argues in the *Village Voice* that McDonald's possesses "the baby face of grown-up greed" (1993, p. 42). Several years ago a Burger Chef manager met and exchanged pleasantries with a man who he assumed was the new manager of the McDonald's that had just opened in the area. Proposing that the two hamburger outlets might work out a friendly deal to exchange emergency supplies of beef, buns, and other fast food needs, the Burger Chef manager was startled at the response of the McDonald's employee, Ralph Lanphar. Lanphar identified himself not as a manager, but as an area supervisor, and said: "We're going to run you out of business" (quoted in Love, 1986, p. 113). Indeed, McDonald's corporate training cultivates such attitudes among its executives (*The Economist*, 1996; Kovel, 1997; Love, 1995).

In the spring of 1955, when Kroc had just purchased the corporation from the McDonald brothers and established his Chicago headquarters, the Chicago School of Economics was establishing itself across town. The concurrence is significant, for McDonald's aggressive policies would be justified by the Chicago prophets of the free market. Many of the Chicago economists, including the Nobel Prize–winners

Milton Friedman, Theodore Schultz, and George Stigler, were teaching students around the world about the merits of unregulated business and the movement of power from the governmental public sector to the corporate private sector. The two Chicago-based institutions were permanently linked, as the economists' theories helped create a global economy that would facilitate McDonald's massive, worldwide expansion and McDonald's came to symbolize the success of the free market.

By the end of the twentieth century, only a couple of countries in the world community would be working against global economics Chicago style, and McDonald's would be operating in over a hundred countries. Most of the world's banks, international financial institutions, and global organizations would subscribe to neo-classical economics, and McDonald's would serve over 35 million individuals per day. As a result of such factors, multinational corporate power was becoming so great that national governments could not control it. The dawn of the new millennium would observe tremendous changes in the way the world operated.

According to their own criteria, both the Chicago School and McDonald's were on target. Friedman and the Chicago economists correctly argued that free market policies would stimulate fiscal growth, increased exports, and debt repayment. And Kroc was correct in arguing that his formula of standardization, cleanliness, efficiency, and love-of-America, family-values, child-targeted advertising would make McDonald's a household name. But the Chicago scholars did not concern themselves with the global economy's vulnerability to trouble in any one country, the environmental destruction engendered by a growing world of American-style consumers, and the disparity of wealth between the haves and the have-nots that threatens the security of all.

Kroc and the McDonald's boys did not consider the nutritional and health effects of McDonaldization on children's diet or the effects on the ecosystem of increased beef production or the social impact of the escalating number of low-paid, dead-end, deskilled, and dehumanized jobs. The consequences of the dual Chicago victories are just beginning to reveal themselves: The financial, political, social, ecological, and spiritual toll will be shockingly expensive.

The Battle for the Sign

Because of the success of McDonald's signification process and the American discomfort with discussions of political power, McDonald's has been able to deflect much of the criticism leveled against it over the years. But as the company gains more and more power with less and less regulation, the corporate tolerance for criticism is decreasing. Significantly, corporations have begun to deploy their legal departments to fight unfavorable press (Vidal, 1997). Recent union criticism of particular businesses has been countered by corporate legal departments with charges of "racketeering" and threats of prosecution under the Racketeer Influence and Corrupt Organizations Act (RICO). With their cadres of lawyers and armies of powerful lobbyists, corporations present an imposing threat to critics (Kincheloe, 1999). Kroc, as always, was open about his intolerance of criticism of McDonald's: "I get mad as hell and cuss when someone takes cheap shots at McDonald's or me in print" (quoted in Vidal, 1997, p. 39). Such an attitude was well established in the corporate culture. When contacts in the Special Branch—the division of Britain's police that investigates subversives and international criminals—tipped McDonald's that members of a London Greenpeace organization were criticizing the company, management went into action.

In a case of classic hypersensitivity and overreaction, McDonald's hired two private investigation agencies to infiltrate and spy upon the Greenpeace organization in London. Since neither agency was told that the other had been engaged, the ensuing fiasco was worthy of a *Pink Panther* episode or *Mad Magazine*'s "Spy vs. Spy." Greenpeace meetings were often attended by more spies than members, and spies even stuffed anti-McDonald's mailouts and handed out "What's Wrong with McDonald's" leaflets to the public. This relatively insignificant leaflet would prompt McDonald's executives in Chicago to take its distributors to court for libel. Spending almost twenty million dollars and tying up the courts for almost six years, McDonald's pursued two activists (Helen Steel and David Morris) with no money or jobs (Vidal, 1997). No corporate action better illustrates the power-hunger of international corporations and their desire to be above criticism than the McLibel trial. As a symbol of the emerging corporate order, McLibel should make us pause and think about the future of civil liberties.

As much as anything else, McLibel was a battle for sign value between a corporation buoyed by an advertising budget of almost two billion dollars a year and an ad hoc support campaign that raised about twenty-five thousand dollars over a four-year period. Fighting every sentence printed in the leaflet, McDonald's ensnared itself and the defendants in a legal quagmire of legendary proportions. It seems that no one in McDonald's management expected anyone to contest the suit. When Steel and Morris mounted a defense based on the company's history of social irresponsibility, the expensive legal team McDonald's had assembled was unprepared. David (Morris) had outflanked

Goliath. Thus, the trial was a circus of postmodern capitalism, a spectacle worthy of the era. Fact was matched by counter-fact, assertion by counter-assertion, as the trial dragged on throughout the 1990s (Vidal, 1997). Its spectacular dynamic, its World Wrestling Federation–style David-versus-Goliath ambiance, and the energy of Morris and Steel's anticorporate supporters attracted attention. With its verbal war of ideologies and cultures, the legal saga could have become a great movie of the week. But McDonald's is simply too powerful to let *that* PR disaster happen.

4 McDonald's as Cultural Pedagogy

We watch McDonald's send scouts to new lands, agents to communicate with the locals to try to avoid clashes, and officers to fend off attacks on the Golden Arches. McDonald's public relations spokesperson Terri Capatosto, referring to the company's attempts at international expansion, states: "The pioneers take all the arrows" (*CQ Researcher*, 1991, p. 831). Business leaders' language underscores the idea of the multinational corporation as part of the new colonialism. In the New World Order, brute political and economic force, while necessary, is insufficient. The hearts and minds of the colonized peoples must be courted and won if corporate colonization is to work. This is why cultural pedagogy is so important—people must be subtly and adeptly taught to accept not just the corporate presence, but the ideologies, such as Chicago School neo-classical economics, that support corporate power. In nearly every industrialized country, the impact of corporate cultural pedagogy has helped move citizens away from traditional politics toward corporate-financed right-wing populism.

As the old political structures fall apart, Ronald McDonald—son of Adam Smith by Ray Kroc—becomes a symbol of the victors of the ideological struggles of the last 150 years. Magazines and newspapers around the world have pictorially depicted this concept again and again with shots of

Ronald at the Kremlin, Ronald at Tiananmen Square, Ronald with Polish schoolchildren, and Ronald with a Ukrainian woman eating a Big Mac at the gates of Kiev. The semiotic inscription of the corporate victory over state socialism is observable in each picture. Journalists gush about McDonald's "global clout," citing *The Economist*'s Big Mac Index, which monitors the price of a Big Mac in 33 selected countries. Many business journalists and economic analysts call the index an amazingly accurate guide to whether national currencies are overvalued or undervalued on the world market (Hamilton, 1997; Hundley, 1997; Martin and Schumann, 1997).

Some contemporary analysts bring back the colonial specter of the White Man's Burden, equating McDonald's influence on colonized peoples with the "civilizing" missions of the European explorers of previous centuries. Anthropologist John Watson (1997c) writes of McDonald's burden in Hong Kong:

> Courtesy toward strangers was largely unknown in the 1960s: boarding a bus during rush hour could be a nightmare and transacting business at a bank teller's window required brute strength. Many people credit McDonald's with being the first public institution in Hong Kong to enforce queuing, and thereby helping to create a more "civilized" social order. (p. 94)

The uncritical acceptance of corporate power in Watson's description is striking in light of the historical relationship between Western colonists and the Chinese—and Asians in general. In the early 1990s, South Koreans and McDonald's conducted trade negotiations with the support of U.S. trade representatives. During this period the South Korean Ministry of Agriculture, Forestry, and Fishing and other commercial organizations developed a poster to encourage

Koreans to consume domestic products. Portraying a huge grain of rice conquering a fatty hamburger, the placard read: "Healthy eating equals eating Korean rice." Exercising their colonizing power, McDonald's representatives and the U.S. trade delegation told the Koreans that they found the representation offensive and an unfair impediment to free trade between South Korea and the United States. The sign was never displayed again, as the South Koreans bowed to multinational corporate power couched in the discourse of the unassailable demands of the free market—the unimpeachable imperative of free trade (Bak, 1997).

Crossing the Sea of Japan to the Japanese McDonald's empire, the company could always count on Kroc's eastern soulmate, Den Fujita, to set things straight. Like his American mentor, Fujita never minced his words. His job, he told the press, was to Westernize the palate of Japanese children, to hook kids on hamburgers for life. McDonald's cultural pedagogy has worked so well in Fujita's Japan that per capita beef consumption has dramatically increased and the Japanese Ministry of Education has noted that children are losing their facility with chopsticks. Because of these dynamics, the weight of the Japanese people is rising. "That is a good tendency," Fujita exclaims. "Japanese must be bigger and taller" (quoted in Katayama, 1986, p. 116).

One of the most unexpected manifestations of McDonald's corporate colonialism was the company's victory in France, with its tradition of fine cuisine. Analysts argued that McDonald's hamburgers would disgust the French palate. McDonald's may be powerful, they contended, but it could never penetrate the French market. To travel in contemporary France is to recognize the shortsightedness of such prognostications. A short walk down the Champs Elysees will turn up five McDonald's within a few hundred yards of each other. A McDonald's stands near the Palace of Versailles, where hamburger wrappers swirl around an otherwise clean street and sidewalk. On the inside wall of that outlet is painted a mural of Napoleon and an army consisting of Ronald McDonald, the Hamburglar, and other McDonaldland characters. Even the French have succumbed to the colonizing power of McDonald's cultural pedagogy.

McDonald's formula for success is taught in seminars all over the world by free market gurus advocating nomadic corporate colonization free of governmental regulations and social responsibility. These economists understand that control of nations and states may no longer be necessary in the current sociocultural climate. This statement is not meant to imply that corporations do not want to own the state—they do. The point is that most of the corporate work in hyperreality can be accomplished through cultural pedagogy operating on the terrain of everyday life. A victory on this level preempts the relevance of governmental power because cognitive and emotional vectors of people's lives have already been colonized. When power through the use of media can penetrate to this intrapsychic level, we have entered into a new dimension of cultural life.

This dynamic is illustrated in China, where the power of popular cultural pedagogy has taken precedence over state power. Chinese Communist officials waged a concerted rational campaign against McDonald's in the state-controlled press. The food is inedible and unaffordable, state leaders argued, as they threatened to evict McDonald's from the country (Kaye, 1992; Tefft, 1994). Meanwhile, Beijing residents lined up for McDonald's fare. The corporate pedagogy worked; the biggest problem the Chinese McDonald's had in its early years was dealing with the crowds and the traffic gridlock surrounding its outlets. Eventually, Chinese officials recognized that they had lost the battle and negotiated an "understanding" that would allow McDonald's to maintain its operations. Again the cultural pedagogy of affect and emotion revealed its power to shape the world.

Legitimizing Corporatism: The Re-education of the Public

Throughout the twentieth century, corporations in America produced educational/advertising campaigns to legitimate their activities. From the 1930s through the 1950s, campaigns touted the virtues of private property and the free enterprise system. In the 1930s businesses produced advertisements designed to counter "radical elements" in the country dedicated to undermining capitalism (Neilson, 1999). Having felt the sting of public criticism in the late 1960s, corporations began in the early 1970s to produce a series of so-called legitimation ads to improve their public image. Most of these ads, from the 1930s through the 1970s, were similar in style to the Chinese government's attacks on McDonald's: They provided rational arguments, in this case for the benefits of free enterprise economics. Later, gaining insight into new forms of public persuasion from advertising agencies and from the handlers of Ronald Reagan's political career, corporations began to present their appeals for public support less rationally and more emotionally and semantically. Indeed, it became harder and harder to tell the difference between Reagan-era political appeals and advertisements for General Motors, Mobil Oil, Miller Beer, Beatrice Corporation, and McDonald's. Where Reagan was surrounded by images of sunrises, horses, and amber waves of grain, McDonald's was connected to loving families, sandlot baseball, and early twentieth-century small-town America.

Just as Reagan did not have to offer detailed political positions in his campaign ads, corporations and their ad agencies realized that the persuasive messages they wanted to deliver could be encoded in an emotionally evocative narrative. The corporate campaigns used the language of pedagogy; the public, corporate leaders contended, needed to be "educated" about the virtues of privately owned business. From the early seventies onward, corporate spending for legitimation ads increased every year: in 1971, $157.6 million; in 1977, $329.3 million; in 1989, $1.4 billion. An ever-growing percentage of these expenditures were for television advertising, which, corporate leaders confided, was better at engendering emotion and embedding simple messages in the public consciousness (Goldman and Papson, 1996).

Throughout the 1990s corporate advertising budgets continued to expand, as did the percentage of advertising shown on television. Thus, a corporate curriculum had been developed, designed, as Michael Apple (1996) puts it, to create the biggest public re-education campaign in American history. McDonald's has played an important role in the re-education campaign with advertising that undermines individual and collective meanings that contradict the curriculum the company wishes to teach about its good citizenship, its 100 percent Americanism, and its embrace of traditional moral virtue. As McDonald's and other corporations' globalization efforts expand, this cultural pedagogy of corporate legitimation takes on new dimensions. One of the key goals of McDonald's foreign marketing involves the promotion of corporate values and culture. Thus, the effort to promote a specific set of political positions and educate the public to accept them is taking place on a global level.

The success of the legitimation ads is disturbing on both political and moral levels. As more and more citizens consented to the legitimacy of corporate behavior, they began to believe that it was society's responsibility to help create a "good business climate." More people than ever before accepted economic inequality as a necessary feature of the economy, and inequality expanded. The income of the poor fell, while that of the rich increased. U.S. corporations paid 26 percent of all local, state, and federal taxes in 1950, but only 8 percent by the 1990s (Kincheloe, 1999). Corporate offensives against labor unions (with McDonald's leading the charge), the establishment of caps on the minimum wage, adoption of exploitative practices such as the utilization of part-time and third-world labor (usually women and minorities), and reinstitution of patriarchal sweatshops have become the order of the day. Such developments undermine the stability of the middle class, since an ever-increasing percentage of new jobs are in the low-wage category—McJobs (Associated Press, 1998; Affleck, 1998; Yakabuski, 1997). A growing number of people are marginal to the work force, accepting "contingent employment" in jobs with few benefits and no assurance of security (Goldman and Papson, 1996; Manning and Cullum-Swan, 1994; *Personnel Journal*, 1994).

New technologies, computerization, and automation displaced workers from jobs in the industrial sector. As the changing economy moved workers from industrial and agricultural jobs to service and information employment, many men and women watched their middle-class status disappear. McDonald's and other fast food companies continue to work on automation strategies to reduce their already-low labor costs. These downsizing strategies have affected middle-level and semiskilled jobs (especially those in the nine-to 12-dollar-an-hour range), resulting in further economic bi-polarization, but enhancing the good business climates that corporate cultural pedagogy insists are essential to the health of the nation and now the world (Block, 1990; Grossberg, 1992; Kellner, 1989).

When examined, the components of a neo-liberal good business climate may not be in everyone's interest. Who exactly benefits from lower labor costs, less unionization, and reduced governmental protection of workers (Kincheloe, 1995, 1999)? In many ways the corporate curriculum has been phenomenally successful, inducing individuals around the world to buy into policies that are clearly not in their best interests. Using emotional appeals, corporations have persuaded more and more world citizens to trust them. It is corporations, according to the ads, that bring contentment, the good things of life, and Happy Meals to us, our loved ones, and our children. Who could cast stones at such sacred institutions? The anger some of my questions evoked from interviewees is testimony to the success of the corporate re-education program. When asked to respond to the McLibel court decision about McDonald's manipulation of children through its ads, a 25-year-old mother of two from New York exploded:

> I am so sick of these liberal do-gooders bashing corporations. McDonald's is not manipulating kids. It's called THE FREE ENTERPRISE SYSTEM, if you don't know. You communists wouldn't understand that. McDonald's is making a profit, and people like you just can't stand that. You want the government to run this and the government to run that. McDonald's appeals to kids, and you want to make government even bigger so we can censor these ads. Don't talk to me about McDonald's advertisements. Go get a job in the USSR—oops, it doesn't exist any more. I guess, professor, people like you are just out of luck. (Interview, 1998)

Winning the Cold War: McDonald's Re-educates the Commies

All human problems, the corporate curriculum instructs, have a commodity solution. Are you harried and stressed by the pace of contemporary life? You deserve a break today. So, get up and get away to McDonald's. How can we treat the providers of joy and happiness as anything other than special? "It's called THE FREE ENTERPRISE SYSTEM." If they want a good business climate, give them what they want. They give us what *we* want, after all.

This dynamic finds expression around the world in the most unlikely places. According to Yunxiang Yan (1997) a Chinese newspaper recently ran a story about a couple in their early seventies coming to a Beijing McDonald's to celebrate National Day—an important Chinese holiday. Reading the newspaper article, one would think it was a run-of-the-mill Communist propaganda piece about the *tu* (the antiquated and backward) of the old China and the *yang* (the fashionable, progressive, and foreign—connected to the West) of the new China. Two pictures of the couple appear: One, taken in 1949, depicts a gaunt, undernourished pair; the other, taken in front of the Beijing McDonald's, shows them as healthy and fashionably attired (Yan, 1997, p. 41). The article is anything but a typical Chinese propaganda piece, for in it McDonald's signifies the progressive nature of contemporary life in China. It was McDonald's, a capitalist, American institution, that made everyday living in China in the 1990s worthwhile. The pedagogy of the commodity solution is successful even in a state uncomfortable with the ideology of the market. It takes a powerful pedagogy to cross that ideological barrier.

By attaching signifiers of joy, Americana, and contemporaneousness to its public image, McDonald's gains unexpected benefits from its pedagogy. Even with the low wages it offers, McDonald's can expect many young people in China and other countries to apply for jobs, for it is commonly believed that such work prepares them for modern jobs in a globalized economy. The modernization signifier emerges yet again. In a society where parents are obsessed with their children's education, McDonald's cultural pedagogy of signification induces them to bring those children to McDonald's for a lesson in the modernization it represents.

To further exploit this tendency, McDonald's in China promotes a learning environment by providing paper and pens to children as they enter the restaurant, sponsoring essay contests, presenting children's programs in the restaurants, and celebrating "Teachers' Day" with gifts and certificates of merit for teachers (Yan, 1997). In Taiwan many schools allow parents or children to order lunches from McDonald's to be delivered directly to the school. Many Taiwanese school personnel see the practice as educational, teaching students the "hygienic behavior and proper etiquette" that will serve them well in the globalized workplace of the future (Wu, 1997, p. 133). McDonald's in these contexts has successfully transformed itself in the public mind from a fast food restaurant to a "public" educational institution that supports parents' career aspirations for their children (Deetz, 1993; Goldman and Papson, 1996).

What we are watching here is the successful propagation of a politics of neo-classical economics. The Chicago connection emerges again: Chicago School economics made McDonald's global growth possible, and McDonald's spreads the Chicago ideology once it gains a foothold in a new country. Many nations are just beginning to discover that the effects of the free market ideology may not live up to the hype, for in addition to the labor-unfriendliness and inequality of wealth produced in good times, a worldwide "free market recession" is always hovering on the horizon. McDonald's future is inexorably tied to the success or failure of globalized neo-classical economics. In many of the interviews I conducted, a correlation emerged between frequent and enthusiastic patronizing of McDonald's and a positive view of an unrestricted market capitalism, contemporary business behavior, or both. Some McDonaphiles were willing to argue that God created the free enterprise system and that McDonald's was doing the Lord's work:

> I know Jesus Christ believed in the free enterprise system—there are many references to it in the Bible. Ray Kroc was a man of God and through McDonald's he carried on the Lord's work. I thank God for men like him, praising Jesus through the free enterprise system. I'm proud to eat at McDonald's. (Interview, 1992)

Thus, some customers darkening the glass doors of Kroc's Kingdom are thereby proclaiming their belief in the free enterprise system. It is easy to understand the appeal of McDonald's pedagogy, the simplicity of the franchising plan that made Kroc a capitalist icon, the seductiveness of the notion that "if Kroc could do it, then, by God, so could I." Indeed, some of the patrons I observed under the Golden Arches were taking ideological communion: They were eating Adam Smith.

This dimension of McDonald's achieves the highest clarity when the North American press writes of McDonald's presence in former Communist countries. A journalist for *Mademoiselle* maintained that Muscovites have not seen a line as long as the one to the new McDonald's "since Lenin's tomb went out of fashion." All the members of the line wanted only one thing, he concluded: "The tastes of capitalism on a sesame-seed bun" (Bastable, 1993, p. 98). Other writers in the popular press picked up on this "a-taste-of-capitalism-for-hungry-Commies" motif, describing the eagerness of Russians, Hungarians, Yugoslavs, Chinese, and other peoples from "behind the Iron Curtain" for the Big Mac (e.g., Wood and Wilson-Smith, 1988, p. 30). In this context the idea emerged in the American media that Ronald McDonald kicked the Commies' ass, leading one front of the charge that won the Cold War.

Since one is never sure where Ronald McDonald ends and Ray Kroc begins, Ronald's role in the Cold War is morphed onto the memory of capitalist entrepreneurial genius Kroc. It was Ray Kroc and the inspired corporate innovators that he represents, journalists wrote, who, along with Ronald Reagan and his military resolve, won the Cold War (Feder, 1997). Thus, the semiotic connection to Americana was extended in a manner that Kroc could only have dreamed about. Kroc and his McDonald's were connected to John Wayne, Reagan, Ollie North and the Marines, Charlton Heston and the National Rifle Association as members of the iconic dreamscape of the American Right. A hamburger is indeed more than a hamburger: You get two all-beef patties, special sauce, lettuce, cheese, onions, pickles, and *ideology* on a sesame seed bun.

The pedagogy takes place at all levels—the macro-ideological and the micro-disciplinary—as in most educational systems. American schools have historically provided a macro-ideology of American-style democracy and capitalism while developing disciplinary means of controlling individual students to achieve order. Teaching a market fundamentalism that abandons the social-democratic notion of material security for all, McDonald's and its corporate compadres and political supporters have to develop an especially effective disciplinary power. Make no mistake; the numerous losers in the market-driven global economy, both in the United States and around the world, will eventually get very angry.

So far, however, McDonald's has displayed an uncanny ability to teach people in diverse cultures through television and other marketing devices to eat alien food, even to change their traditional diet. This is no small feat. The company has successfully taught people how to order and eat in a fast food restaurant—a major educational task often accomplished with handouts, pictorial lessons, and verbal guidance (Watson, 1997c). As for worker training, many company executives have begun to claim that McDonald's has taken over the social role the army used to play: teaching young people "discipline, teamwork, and routine" (Vidal, 1997, p. 38). When one out of 10 Americans and a growing number of world citizens get their first job at McDonald's, the power of the corporation's pedagogy becomes even greater (ibid.).

Why Know This? Resisting the Power of McDonald's

It is important to know about the power of McDonald's and other forms of right-wing cultural pedagogy so we can develop forms of resistance to it. As of now, far too few people are either aware of or working against these powerful ideological messages. In a democratic society we need to develop social spaces where we can create critical citizens who have the power to shape their own civic lives via their understanding of the processes of knowledge production and reception. Although the McLibel fiasco has created groups of resisters to McDonald's pedagogy around the world, including organizations such as Kids Against McDonald's, few organizing efforts against corporatist pedagogy in general can be found. A depoliticized hyperreality has led to inertia.

Given the upheavals powerful corporations are causing in people's lives from Pennsylvania to Malaysia, this inertia makes sense only if we view it as a postmodern phenomenon. Just a little analysis reveals McDonald's connections to a multitude of sociocultural, political, economic, and educational issues: nutrition, public health, nationalism, social ethics, global trade, political consciousness, ideology, and others ad infinitum. In the contemporary world of politics, the corporate production of information is where the action is. Political resistance to right-wing free market economic power must focus on these new political conditions in a manner that helps citizens understand the new complexity of the way power operates. Such understanding will enable them to criticize sociopolitical practices and institutions that are now protected from scrutiny. Concerned citizens must infiltrate the corporate culture of power.

The McInformation Network (McSpotlight, 1997) provides a good example of how we can organize to counter the overwhelming pedagogical power of multinational corporations—how McDonald's well-financed legal resources can be overturned for the public good. Our critical vision involves a resistance that takes the libidinal energy/desire that McDonald's and other corporations colonize and deploys it for progressive social and individual change. In the new corporate order, new forms of communication and community are necessary to a politics of resistance. At the beginning of the twenty-first century, it is amazing how few civic organizations offer individuals the possibility for alternative and progressive political action in light of the corporate co-optation of the politics of information. Being able to read the world outside the blinders of corporate disinformation helps ground our resistance. This critical reading recognizes and specifies the way free market fundamentalism has become

a capitalist jihad designed, in the name of freedom, to produce a democratic illiteracy. Given this reality, resistance is
inseparable from the development of literacy in media,
semiotics, and power (Bell and Valentine, 1997; Best and
Kellner, 1991; McLaren, 1997; Vidal, 1997; Wartenberg,
1992).

Literate resisters both "occupy" and undermine the information emanating from corporate and corporate-supported
sources. They become hermeneuts able to read corporate
information around a variety of interpretations and from a
plethora of social and ideological contexts—what this book is
attempting to do. Practitioners could study McDonald's in
light of the politics of information control or in the context of
contemporary concerns with depoliticization. Media/semi-
otic/power literacy helps people from all backgrounds discern the ways in which their histories, social worlds, and
political consciousness may be reconfigured by the information-producers of hyperreality. McDonald's pseudo-histori-
cal, antiqued film footage of a happy late nineteenth-/early
twentieth- century white America of conflict-free small towns
is trying to teach us that the McDonald's corporation is as
much a part of the pantheon of historical American heroes as
George Washington and Abraham Lincoln. Also worth noting
is the implication that this romanticized and untrue pre-1960s
republic, simpler, more natural, crime-free, hard-working,
and morally virtuous, was made possible by the business community. "Can't we just release them from civic responsibility
and senseless 'big-government' taxes and regulations and let
them do their valuable jobs?" the re-educated ask.

One interviewee repeated these lessons to me:

> Why do we have to hear all this talk about social responsibility
> of corporations? In America corporations exist for just one rea-
> son—to turn a profit. Companies like McDonald's should be

free to engage in any activity that helps them turn that profit. In fact *social responsibility* for companies should involve making a profit so they can hire more workers and create more capital. After that a company holds no responsibility to the community. It's done its job. (Interview, 1992)

Sophisticating Resistance: Developing a Power Literacy

So, a burger is not just a burger. Food in general, in the postmodern condition, is not simply about nutrition and life sustenance. And McDonald's transcends ground beef and potatoes to take on political, pedagogical, and cultural meanings. Our eating habits and desire for food tell us about who we are, where we come from, and where we stand (or are placed) in the pecking order of power. The theme emerges again: In order to resist the overwhelming impact of corporate politics, individuals concerned with the development of a just and democratic society must understand how power works; they must develop a power literacy. We often discuss power, but most people are uncertain about what the term means.

A consensus seems to be emerging around the notion that power is a basic component of human existence. At this point, however, consensus dissolves, as analysts run like quail in diverse theoretical directions (Kincheloe and Steinberg, 1997). Power is a fundamental constituent of human reality that shapes both the oppressive and the productive aspects of the human condition. Scholars from the cultural studies tradition tend to accept the thesis that power is a fundamental constituent of reality, embedded in the social framework of race, class, gender, commerce, occupations, communications, and everyday interaction. In this view power is present in all human relationships—the interactions of customers and businesspeople, the sexual lives of lovers, or readers and authors (Bell and Valentine, 1997).

Since power is everywhere, it is not something that can be easily dispensed with or overthrown; I do not propose to "wipe out" McDonald's or corporate power. Simplistic politics that propose to put an end to power relations do not understand power's connection to the construction of social and cultural life (Cooper, 1994; McCarthy, 1992; Musolf, 1992). Power is not simply the unchanging exercise of a binary relationship in which A exercises power over B and B responds by formulating acts of resistance against A. In its complexity and ambiguity, both dominant and subordinate individuals and groups deploy power; it is not the province of one group and not the other. Indeed, we are all empowered and we are all unempowered, in that we all possess abilities and we are all limited in the ability to use them. Thus, conceptions of power that depict it as a one-dimensional unified force with standardized outcomes miss important aspects of its nature. For example, when McDonald's management and other advocates of free market capitalism argue that the market works merely to satisfy needs—that is, that consumer power flows exclusively toward the producers of goods to shape their production decisions—they fail to understand the multidimensional flow of power in real life. The anticorporate McInformation network exerts power; it is not as mighty as McDonald's, but important nonetheless.

Consumer power has traditionally not been sufficient to thwart McDonald's reluctance to publicize data concerning nutrition, environmental aspects of production, cultural insensitivity, and the exploitation of labor. Such information, when it has been accessed, compiled, and released by the McInformation Network and other agencies, has changed the consciousness and behavior of many fast food consumers. A counterhegemonic power circulates around media outlets, is interpreted and connected to various contexts, and is incorporated into various ways of making sense of the sociopolitical world. Thus, power flows, sometimes invisibly, in more than one direction (Bizzell, 1991; Cooper, 1994; Keat, 1994; Rorty, 1992). Power is nothing if not complex, ambiguous, and perplexing—indeed, that is part of its power. In hyperreality, with its information saturation, its effective disguising of the political dimension, and its global media networks, power is everywhere, but nowhere specific. Hidden by the Klingon cloaking device, the effects of power are absent from both individual consciousness and the public conversation.

John Fiske (1993) uses the term "power bloc" to describe the social formations around which power politics operates in contemporary society. Arguing that power-wielders do not constitute a particular class or well-defined social category, Fiske speaks of a power bloc as an ever-shifting set of strategic and tactical social alliances. Such alliances are arranged unsystematically whenever social situations arise that threaten the position of allies, or whenever it is in the interest of the participants in the bloc to support mutually beneficial positions. Power blocs are historically specific, socially specific, and issue-specific; they come and go in relation to changing cultural arrangements. McDonald's, Wendy's, Burger King, Taco Bell, Pizza Hut, and other fast food companies are popularly perceived as competitors in a market sector. On one level, of course, this is true: They often run advertisements attacking one another, or touting their own products over a rival's. From Fiske's power-bloc perspective, however, one can see that when it comes to macro-economic policy, the competitors coalesce into a power bloc for to ensure "good business climates." Pooling their collective political muscle and information-producing capabilities, they exert tremendous influence in political-economic policy.

For Fiske, power "is a systematic set of operations upon people that works to ensure the maintenance of the social order . . . and ensure its smooth running" (1993, p. 11). It stands to reason that the individuals and groups who benefit the most from the maintenance of this social order will align their interests with those of the dominant power system and work to keep it running smoothly. In this context Fiske concludes that the power bloc can be better described by "what it does than what it is" (ibid.). In this configuration the notion of "the people" includes those who fall outside the power bloc and are "disciplined" by it. Falling outside the power bloc does not mean that an individual has no power. Outsiders merely hold a weaker power (Fiske labels it a "localizing power"). Indeed, as we have seen, it is a power that can be cultivated, strengthened, and often successfully deployed. The foundation of a localizing power rests on our notion of power literacy. Defenders of democracy and justice must gain the ability to articulate how cloaked power operates to change the world. The task is extremely difficult but essential at this cultural and political juncture.

In the contemporary globalized society, many observers are distressed by one ever-shifting, ever-realigning, ever-evolving power bloc that unites the corporate culture of McDonald's to a variety of sociocultural, political, and economic groups. These include dominant economic and political elites concerned with securing corporate privilege and enhanced profitability; Social Darwinist conservatives with neo-classical economic perspectives and guardians of so-called traditional American cultural values who advocate a return to "high standards" in schools and the education of workers with higher skills—even they move industries and jobs to Third World locales where workers are often young, female, uneducated, illiterate, and low-cost; upwardly mobile members of the new scientific-technological-managerial ranks, who may be uncomfortable with some of the other members of the power bloc but who join the alliance in pursuit of professional advancement, believing that advancement requires them to buy into corporate management procedures and noncontroversial, conformist identities; and white working-class groups who sense that their white privilege is under attack by government policies like affirmative action and by "pushy minority groups," and who trace what conservatives call the attack on traditional values to immoral African American and Latino welfare recipients, homosexuals, and feminists. The conservative co-optation of this group is particularly distressing, since it is itself often a victim of neo-classical economics and right-wing political policies (Apple, 1996; Fiske, 1993; Hinchey, 1998; Macedo, 1994).

As power literacy is enhanced by an understanding of these ever-shifting power blocs, individuals begin to realize that such an appreciation alone is insufficient. In addition to understanding this macro-dynamic of power, we also need to understand the micro-reception and production of power at the level of the group and the individual. Although the conservative power bloc exerts a profound effect on contemporary socioeconomic and political life, individuals have the agency to join it or resist it. Their choices may be constrained by the information to which they have access, but choices exist nonetheless. As Martin Parker (1998) writes in a response to George Ritzer's *McDonaldization of Society* (1993): "Big Macs are the systematized products of capital but are also consumed as one element in the idiosyncratic and contingent lives of millions of individuals" (p. 11).

Analysis of the intersection of the macro- and the micro-levels around the production and reception of power from both sites is necessary in a critical power literacy. Especially important in this examination of sites of intersection is understanding the libidinal, sensual, and imaginative aspects typically ignored in traditional sociological discourse. By ignoring these social and psychological dimensions of power, traditional rationalistic discourse misses the very ways in which power structures consciousness and shapes individuals' relationship to power blocs.

Recognizing power's colonization of affect and desire, combined with recognizing its use of ideologies to construct rational meanings that support the status quo, gives one a sense of macro-power's double-barreled attempt to colonize the micro-domain of individual consciousness. Such dynamics may appear complex at first glance, but there is absolutely no reason why most people cannot grasp and make use of them in shaping their own civic consciousness and political activity. And then the role of McDonald's in contemporary global life will become clearer and clearer. It will never be simple; there will be no bumper sticker answers to the question of "how to resist." The struggle for justice and democracy would be much easier if resistance were so simple. Just because hyperreality is fragmented, mystified, disjointed, and contradictory, we should not give up the attempt to make sense of it and act in just and egalitarian ways (Peace, 1990). "Resistance is futile," a 2000 McDonald's ad campaign proclaimed, in all its semiotic richness. Nevertheless, a critical power literacy can lead to social change.

Complexity, Yes—Surrender, No

The more complex power, power relations, and the mystification of power become, the more people will give up the fight for social justice. Traditionally, movements have not been built on complexity. It should encourage, not discourage, us to know that the public's reception of McDonald's ideology and its colonization of libido and desire is more complex than many analysts of power previously thought. Just because a powerful social institution controls ideological knowledge production, it does not follow that receivers of the data will fall automatically under its power (Gottdiener, 1995). In his book on McDonald's in East Asia, *Golden Arches East*, anthropologist James Watson (1997c) falls into the trap of giving up on a critical analysis of McDonald's power because of the complexity of its reception.

Watson ignores the size of the McDonald's empire, its profits of nearly $2 billion a year, the 35 million customers it serves each day, its status as the world's largest retail property owner, beef consumer, and chicken purchaser. Such descriptions might be our starting place as we work to demystify the power of such multinational behemoths. Some accounts leave out the role that money plays in the marketing of McDonald's around the world and the nature of the company's relations with state power structures. Some descriptions of the imagery McDonald's uses in its advertising fail to connect it to the commercial interests of television and radio stations and newspapers. Questions about the ideological dynamics and the political impact of such alliances are missing (Kellner, 1990).

As Watson and his coauthors interpret the role of the Golden Arches in Asia, the "localism" of consumer perspectives overturns any macro-social concern with McDonald's power. General analyses of the problems of transnational systems and globalized capitalism are irrelevant in the contemporary political economy, they assert. Local, individually articulated, overt responses to the meaning of corporate activity (such as McDonald's operations in Asia) are the only valid data in this context; indeed, any attempt to discern deeper social, political, and psychological effects of McDonald's information production is somehow misguided. Despite his warning against the tendency to generalize about McDonald's impact in East Asia, Watson concludes his chapter on Hong Kong with the following:

> Having watched the processes of culture change unfold for nearly thirty years, it is apparent to me that the ordinary people of Hong Kong have most assuredly not been stripped of their cultural heritage, nor have they become the uncomprehending dupes of transnational corporations. (Watson, 1997c, pp. 107–8)

When a scholar like John Watson urges us to give up critical analysis because of the complexity of power's effects, he has forgotten a salient question: If corporate legitimation ads do not work, why do McDonald's and other corporations keep spending billions of dollars to keep them on the air? Advertising agencies admit that many of their corporate clients pay them to control the way a political issue connected to corporate interests is framed in the public conversation and the way it will be received by the public: Consider the ads placed by Weyerhaeuser, DuPont, Dow, Phillips Petroleum, and Exxon, for example, concerning environmental issues. Aren't we talking about power and domination here? Aren't we talking about a corporate pedagogy of information control? No doubt people receive and make meaning of these ads in different ways—as people do with all communiqués and texts—but the collective impact cannot be denied. The average person receives four to six hours of media messages per day, and much more if we count corporate-produced messages received at work (Deetz, 1993). Over a couple of decades, the time a person spends receiving ideologically inscribed corporate data expands into tens of thousands of hours. Many people rarely or never hear a perspective countering the intended colonization of emotion/affect or the ideological inscriptions transmitted in these ads.

A series of ads sponsored by the biggest tobacco companies in 1998 told television viewers that attempts to regulate the sale of tobacco and make tobacco companies and smokers pay or share the social and health costs of smoking were misguided. In staged interviews, predominantly working-class Americans repeatedly contended that legislative attempts to reduce smoking and make corporations pay for its human damage were further examples of "big government" interfering with free enterprise. The ads themselves were not that remarkable, but the public reception was so positive that antitobacco legislative efforts were defeated in the U.S. Congress. Power had been wielded via the ideological and affective colonization of viewers with the constructed threat of big government—expressed so well in the phase "you want the government to run this and the government to run that." There is no doubt that different viewers received the tobacco companies' message in different ways and that ethnographic interviews would uncover diametrically conflicting interpretations. Indeed, the reception of the tobacco ads would be complex. Regardless of the complexity of their reception, however, the ads *accomplished their assigned task* of protecting the power and profit margins of companies that make and sell cigarettes. The tobacco companies were simply cashing in on an ideological and affective pedagogy perfected by McDonald's and other corporations over the last few years.

To divert public attention from their expanding power, corporations have inserted into their re-education campaigns an ideological and affective portrait of government as the enemy of the people. Picking up on progressive discontent with the failures of the U.S. government in Vietnam and Watergate, corporations and their political allies represent government as a Big Brother gobbling up our freedoms, and in particular our most basic freedom: the right to free enterprise. The freedom to pursue economic policies without social responsibility has been ideologically, semantically, and affectively equated with freedom of speech and peaceful assembly. The fear of power has been removed from the private space of corporations and diverted to the public space of government—a powerful ideological sleight-of-hand that has changed the course of social, cultural, educational, economic, and political history.

The complex ways in which McDonald's and other corporations have accomplished this re-education first of the American public and now the world is, obviously, a key concern of this book. When this process is at work, consumers are addressed as certain types of people with particular lifestyles who buy certain products, go to the McDonald's drive-through after work, and buy Big Macs for the kids. To surrender to the ads and become the people they want us to be because of the hard-to-fathom complexity of the process—or for any other reason—is unthinkable. For the sake of human dignity we must resist, in the process gaining more and more power to shape our own lives and be our own civic-minded and democratically progressive people.

5 Winning Consent for Capital

To sell its burgers and fries, McDonald's must operate not only as a marketer but also as a cultural broker. It enters the cultural domain when it attempts to connect consumers with the meanings surrounding the Big Mac, the Quarter Pounder, and the late Arch Deluxe and persuade them to construct an identification, an emotional bond, with the levels of pleasure its meanings provide. Their emotional bond with particular meanings of McDonald's is involved with the production of identity, new ways of thinking of "self" among consumers. This productive process reflects the way hegemony operates to encourage consent to dominant signifiers and ideologies.

Briefly defined, "hegemony" is the process of maintaining domination in contemporary democratic societies not through the use of force, but through winning the consent of the people. If hegemony is the larger effort of power-wielders to engage the support of diverse citizens, then dominant or hegemonic ideology involves the cultural forms, the meanings, the rituals, and the representations that produce consent to the status quo and individuals' particular places within it.

Understanding the hegemonic process induces us to view McDonald's and other agents of power in a more textured and complex manner: No one-dimensional ruling class operates to impose top-down, unambiguous domination on "subordinated underlings." McDonald's is always engaged in a process of consensus building and compromise with citizens, attaching its signifiers to prevailing folk beliefs like family values, patriotism, and small-town nostalgia. In this "hegemonic negotiation," McDonald's must understand who consumers are, identify their value structures, and use this knowledge to win their allegiance to McDonald's as a cultural (and political-economic) institution. Thus, McDonald's gives the people much of what they already believe and attaches these emotional investments to its own agenda. In this way it gains entry into the recesses of consciousness construction, as the hegemonic process becomes an important component in the twenty-first century production of subjectivity, of human ways of seeing the world (Kellner, 1990; Goldman and Papson, 1996; Gottdiener, 1995). A cautionary note: This process is never simple, linear, or uncontested. Analysts make a mistake when they portray it as seamless and unambiguous. My effort in this book is to portray the hegemonic logic of McDonald's and its profound impact on globalized culture, but never to overstate the operation of this process in the chaos of the lived world.

McDonald's the vampire sucks local folkways and mores into its corporate bloodstream: Consider the mural at the Versailles McDonald's depicting Napoleon and his army riding with Ronald McDonald, the Hamburglar, and the other male McDonaldland characters. The same hegemonic appropriation can be observed at the Tiananmen Square McDonald's when the company mandates that the Chinese national flag be hoisted every morning in front of the restaurant. On special occasions flag-raising ceremonies are attended by soldiers of the People's Liberation Army (Yan, 1997).

Hegemonic appropriation of sociocultural and political values may take on dramatically different forms in different societies. To engage the emotional investments of Americans and Chinese, McDonald's may attach itself to diametrically opposed social and political systems—in China the trappings of the Communist revolution and the totalitarian state, in the United States free enterprise economics and images of a decentralized, family-oriented culture. McDonald's attempts to hide such overt contradictions from worldwide consumers. No McDonald's promotional literature produced for U.S. consumption references the celebration of the Chinese flag at the Beijing outlet. Such knowledge might evoke a new view of McDonald's yellow and red trademark colors among more conservative U.S. citizens, who identify the company with the red, white, and blue.

The culture of power framed in terms of corporate hegemony is a controversial concept. In his preface to *Golden Arches East: McDonald's in East Asia*, anthropologist James Watson (1997a) writes that critical intellectuals vilify McDonald's as an agent of cultural homogenization. McDonald's does not produce cultural homogenization, Watson asserts; nor is it a power-wielding agent of cultural imperialism. As he puts it in his introduction (1997b), critical scholars assume that McDonald's customers

> know what is expected of them, that they have been educated, or disciplined, to behave like "proper" consumers in a modern economy. Scholars who support the cultural imperialism hypothesis would argue that the goal is to turn Russians, Chinese, and Saudis into Americans. As we shall see, however, corporate campaigns to modify consumer behavior do not always go according to plan. (p. 27)

From Watson's perspective, researchers who attempt to delineate corporate hegemony in the globalized world are looking for something that does not exist. His concern with cultural homogenization blinds him to the subtler effects of

McDonald's power and the ways in which it wins consent in different cultural settings. Indeed, what he sees as an absence of cultural homogenization might be read as the success of McDonald's hegemonic activities in foreign venues. Simply put, Watson does not understand hegemony.

According to the view I present here, McDonald's gains its power precisely by *not* attempting to turn Russians, Chinese, and Saudis into Americans. Instead, it works to gain consent by employing cultural beliefs important to the society in which it is operating. Not only is the Chinese (not the American) flag raised at McDonald's outlets in China, but the Chicken McNuggets come with Sichuan dipping sauce. Writing in *Dissent*, Jeffrey Wasserstrom (1998) used Watson's " wonderful new book" to support his own tirade against scholars who would argue that McDonald's and other American corporations are Americanizing and thus homogenizing China. Not once does Wasserstrom's article refer to the power of McDonald's and other American multinational corporations to ideologically influence China, or any other society for that matter.

Nor do Watson and Wasserstrom ask questions about the hegemonic process's use of pleasure and desire to win consent to particular viewpoints and sociopolitical and economic practices. Previous analyses of McDonald's production of pleasure and colonization of desire did not know exactly what to do with these concepts. George Ritzer, for example, operating from a rather high-culture, haute cuisine view of McDonald's debased aesthetic, was concerned with the "illusion of fun" individuals obtained at McDonald's (Parker, 1998). In ignoring the relationship between hegemony and desire, Ritzer, Watson, and others lose sight of the complex interaction between macrosociopolitical and economic structures on one hand and

human agency, the capacity for self-direction, and the production of subjectivity on the other (Miles, 1998). Thus
Watson (1997c) contends that because the children of Hong
Kong do not perceive McDonald's as an alien institution
and have made it their own place of fun, cultural imperialism has been successfully resisted. If Hong Kong youngsters
viewed McDonald's as an alien presence, of course, the
restaurant, and everything it represents, might not succeed
on any level. After 30 years of McDonald's, he concludes,
Hong Kongians "have most assuredly not been stripped of
their cultural heritage" (pp. 107–8), "proving" once again
the irrelevance of critical power analysis.

In these interpretations an individualistic focus on a
sociopolitical phenomenon has erased power. Domination in
the globalized economy is now irrelevant as multinational
corporate nomads wander from country to country simply
providing the trappings of a better life for those who would
consume their products and the meanings that surround
them. Is it possible that individuals might not be able to articulate in precise terms the ways in which signifiers operate in
their lives? Could it be that ethnographers unconcerned with
power and domination might not develop the methodolog-
ical tools to capture the ambiguous and subtle ways such
hegemonic dynamics operate in the context of desire and
pleasure? Is there a connection between the desiring consumer and the notion that American corporations and the
free enterprise ideological aura surrounding them have
latched on to his or her desire? In this context hegemonic
ideology is inscribed not along the explicit lines of rational
persuasion (as is traditionally assumed), but around the
implicit, tenuous connection with pleasure and desire (Best
and Kellner, 1991). A traditional ethnographic interview that
assumes the rationalistic process and asks, "How does the

ideology of the Big Mac influence you politically?" is not going to expose the often obscured and unconscious process at work. Ethnographies of the culture of power must operate at a much more subtle and rigorous level.

Many traditional analyses of McDonald's fail because they neglect the importance of the unconscious and the complex relationships connecting the unconscious and identity to the dynamics of pleasure and desire. The signifiers of Americana, the legitimacy of free market economics, and the lure of modernity are all operating in the Chinese people's interactions with McDonald's. Desire does not exist in isolation from the materiality of the lived world. A burger is more than a burger after all, even in Beijing—and this is important even if everyone does not process the meanings in the same way. On a variety of levels this hegemonic linking of desire to the modernity of McDonald's sets off a cultural process that calls into question precorporatized ways of life. In my interviews with people around the world, I discovered time and again that the world from which many of respondents emerged looked quite primitive to them when viewed through the golden lenses of the McDonald's arches. In fact such a framing elicited embarrassment and fear of identification by moderns as a rube or a hick. Such dynamics reflect the importance of feeling and emotion, the centrality of desire, in the complex workings of power.

The McDonald's experience helps create new material and psychological experiences, especially for individuals who are enculturated outside the confines of Western middle- or upper-middle-class modernity. McDonald's power to tap into desires and create new material and psychological experiences is so great among such people that many Chinese parents think the company puts a secret ingredient in its burgers (Yan, 1997). American parents often laugh when they hear this, acutely understanding the feelings of their Chinese counterparts: Nothing that they know of could evoke such powerful reactions from their children. Through such responses to McDonald's we gain insight into the way the politics of postmodernity operates. Indeed, there is more going on at McDonald's and other sites on the new terrain than Ritzer's analysis of rationalization, Watson's formal ethnographic interviews, or Wasserstrom's understanding of the diversity of perceptions of the firm might indicate.

This is why advertising agencies holding the McDonald's account speak of creating music to situate the hamburger as possessing magical qualities. We have attempted, they confide, to inspire a "feeling . . . an urge to get away from what you ordinarily do" (Boas and Chain, 1976, p. 127). Such songs, described by many observers as highly seductive, contribute to a politics of affect and desire, an emotionally grounded hegemony that induces a young Chinese boy to dream of huge boxes of hamburgers that he could eat every day and other children to fantasize about opening a McDonald's restaurant when they grow up (Yan, 1997). These children's political perspectives, world views, visions of success, and self-images will never be the same.

Corporate Coitus: The Hegemony of Pleasure

To extend its hegemonic power via an ideology of pleasure, in January 1997 McDonald's signed a 10-year agreement with Disney for the exclusive right to use Disney products in its promotions (Hamilton, 1997). The agreement ties together the two pleasure-producing icons in a way that precludes Burger King (for example) from repeating its success with toys linked to the Disney-produced *Pocahontas* (*The Economist*, 1996). (Providing Pocahontas toys and paraphernalia increased same-store revenues for Burger King outlets 10 percent; see Benezra, 1995.) If the key to McDonald's power involves colonizing affect and emotion by producing pleasure, then the company must make sure that it attaches itself to pleasure-producing corporate partners. In addition to Disney, McDonald's has worked with EMI Records Group to sell special compilations of recordings by Garth Brooks, Tina Turner, and Elton John with the purchase of burgers and fries (Morris, 1994). When these recordings were combined with two regional compilations of Latin music and hip-hop, McDonald's sold over nine million albums in a one-month promotion in the mid-1990s (Newman, 1994). At various times the company has crawled into bed with movie distributors to attach low-priced videocassettes to the purchase of a Big Mac–type large sandwich, fries, and a Coke (Bessman, 1989).

One of McDonald's most successful promotions involves Teenie Beanie Babies. This toy is a miniature version of Beanie Babies, an animal-shaped bean bag that is difficult to purchase because of purposefully limited production. In several incarnations of the promotion, customers run to outlets to get free Teenie Beanie Babies with the purchase of a Happy Meal. To increase its sales McDonald's typically releases only a couple of the Beanie pantheon—Patti Platypus, Speedy Turtle, Lizzy Lizard, for example—per week. So popular are the toys that outlets often run out before the end of the seven-day run. I observed lines extending outside restaurants and traffic jams in the middle of weekday afternoons, as mothers and fathers stood in line for hours to obtain the newly released Teenie Beanie Baby. The parents I talked to and observed seemed as excited by the toys as their children. The emotion engendered by the Beanie Babies is profound, and entire subcultures and cyber-communities have grown up around them. The only problem

McDonald's has experienced during these promotions involves reports of parents purchasing Happy Meals only to get the free toys and then dumping the meals.

McDonald's ability to tap into the emotions and affect of different audiences has made it a business-school model for financial success and sociopolitical power. If hegemony means inducing individuals to give their consent to power, then McDonald's is a masterful hegemonizer. One of the most successful strategies for engaging children's consent via the production of pleasure revolves around the McDonaldland characters. Appearing in animated and other television commercials, as statues in McDonald's playgrounds, as pictures on cookie boxes and plastic soft-drink cups, the McDonaldland characters have been inserted into children's everyday lives. The McDonaldland promotions serve as hegemonic myths for a postmodern globalized world—and, disturbingly, they are typically directed at children. To gain a thick understanding of the hegemonic mythic aspects of McDonaldland, one must appreciate the sociopsychological complexity of the characters' "father," Ray Kroc.

Born in 1902 in a working-class neighborhood on the West Side of Chicago, into what he called a "bohunk" (Bohemian) family, Kroc was obsessed throughout his life with proving his worth as both a human being and a businessman (Boas and Chain, 1976). Having failed in several business ventures in his twenties and thirties, Kroc had much to prove by the time the McDonald's opportunity confronted him at the age of 52 (Kroc, 1977, chap. 4). Kroc defined McDonaldland the same way he defined himself—through consumption. Driven by an ambition to own nice things, Kroc peppered his autobiography with references to consumption: "I used to comb through the advertisements in the local newspaper for notices of house sales in the wealthier suburbs. . . . I haunted these sales and picked up pieces of elegant furniture" (Kroc, 1977, p. 27). Watched over by the messianic Ronald McDonald, McDonaldland is a place (your kind of place) where consumption is not only the sole occupation but the means through which its inhabitants gain their identities—the pleasure-based hegemonic ideology of consumption.

McDonaldland is a kid's text fused with Kroc's psyche that reveals itself as an effort to sell the system, to justify consumption as a way of life, to win children's consent to McDonald's culture of power. As the central figure in McDonaldland, Ronald McDonald emerges as a multidimensional clown deity, virgin-born son of Adam Smith, press secretary for the ideology of free enterprise capitalism. He is also Ray Kroc's projection of himself, his ego creation, the most beloved prophet of utopian consumption in the McWorld.

Ronald's life history begins in Washington, D.C., with Willard Scott, the *Today Show* weatherman. Struggling to make it as a junior announcer at WRC-TV in Washington in the early 1960s, Scott agreed to play Bozo the Clown on the station's kid show. When Scott donned the clown suit, he was transformed from Clark Kent to Superman, from bumbling Willard to superclown. The local McDonald's franchisees recognized Scott's talent and employed Bozo as a spokesperson for McDonald's. When the Bozo show was canceled by WRC, McDonald's lost a very effective advertisement. The local McDonald's owners worked with Scott to create Ronald McDonald (Scott's idea), who debuted in October 1963. Ronald was so successful, creating traffic jams every time he appeared in public, that the local operators suggested to the Chicago headquarters that Ronald go national (Love, 1986).

After a lengthy debate over whether they should employ Ronald McDonald as a clown, a cowboy, or a spaceman, corporate leaders and advertisers settled on the clown Ronald. Dumping Scott because he was deemed too fat for the image they wanted to promote (Love, 1986), the company in 1965 hired Coco, an internationally known clown with the Ringling Brothers, Barnum and Bailey Circus. The deification of Ronald began with his first national appearance in the Macy's Thanksgiving Day Parade on November 25, 1966. The press releases issued by the McDonald's Customer Relations Center are canonization documents crosspollinated with frontier tall-tale boasting. "Since 1963, Ronald McDonald has become a household name, more famous than Lassie or the Easter Bunny, and second only to Santa Claus" (McDonald's Customer Relations Center, 1994). All-American twentieth-century Ronald "More famous than Lassie" McDonald meets All-American nineteenth-century Pecos "I have lassoed the tornado" Bill in time-traveling WWF Wrestling.

All of the other characters in McDonaldland, the company's promotional literature reports, revere Ronald—a.k.a. Kroc. He is "intelligent and sensitive . . . he can do nearly anything . . . Ronald McDonald is the *star*" (ibid.). If children are sick, the promos contend, Ronald is there. Even though he has become "an international hero and celebrity" (ibid.), Ronald is still the same friend of children he was in 1963. Ninety-six percent of all children can identify him, according to the early 1960s "Ronald McDonald Awareness Study" fed to the press and described as bogus by the company's unauthorized biographers (Boas and Chain, 1976, pp. 115–16). Ronald was everything Kroc wanted to be: a beloved humanitarian, an international celebrity, a philanthropist, and a musician. Kroc made his living for a while as a piano-player;

Ronald—along with the other McDonaldland characters—entered into a deal with Kid Rhino Records to produce a children's recording. Produced by Mark Volman and Howard Kaylan, formerly of the sixties band The Turtles, the album contained original songs and "classic hits" (McCormick, 1993). Even sophisticates loved Ronald, Kroc wrote in his autobiography (1977, p. 160); Kroc himself would have to experience their affection vicariously through Ronald. Abe Lincoln, too, had been rejected by the sophisticates of his day; as a twentieth-century Lincoln, Kroc prominently displayed a bust of Ronald adjacent to the bust of Lincoln behind his desk at the Chicago headquarters (Kroc, 1977).

According to promotional literature designed for elementary schools, Ronald "became a citizen of [McDonald's] International Division" in 1969 and soon began to appear on television around the world. Kroc was propelled to a new level of celebrity as the corporation "penetrated" the global market. Now known everywhere on earth, Kroc/Ronald became the grand Salesman, the successful postindustrial Willie Loman—they love me in Moscow, Belgrade, and New York. Stung by a plethora of critics, Kroc was obsessed with being perceived as a moral man with a moral company that exerted a wholesome influence on children around the world. Kroc wrote and spoke of his noble calling, establishing franchised "missions" as part of his neo-white man's ideological burden. I provide an humanitarian service, Kroc proclaimed: "I go out and check out a piece of property [that's] not producing a damned thing for anybody," he wrote in his epistles from California. The new franchise provides a better life for scores of people—"out of that bare ground comes a store that does, say, a million dollars a year in business. Let me tell you, it's a great satisfaction to see that happen" (Kroc, 1977, pp. 176–77). Kroc/Ronald McDonald came to personify the great success story of twentieth-century capitalism. Kroc's and his franchises' fortunes came to exemplify the hegemonic ideological notion of what happens when one works hard in the free enterprise system. Kroc/Ronald could win your consent to the process because you envied the financial success they had achieved.

The convergence of the growth of international megacorporations with the expanding technological sophistication of the media has prompted a new era of consumption. Many argue that the postmodern lifestyle revolves around the act of consuming (Grossberg, 1992). In McDonaldland, Ronald McDonald serves as CEO/archduke over his fiefdom of consumer junkies. The Hamburglar's addiction to hamburgers is "cute." According to the literature the company provides to schoolchildren, the Hamburglar's "main purpose in life is the acquisition of McDonald's hamburgers." Grimace is described as "generous and affectionate . . . [his] primary personality attribute is his love for McDonald's shakes." Captain Crook's most important passion is his love of McDonald's Filet-O-Fish sandwiches (McDonald's Customer Relations Center, 1994).

As a free enterprise utopia, McDonaldland erases all differences, all conflicts; social inequities are overcome through acts of consumption. As such hegemonic messages justify existing power relations, conformity emerges as the logical path to self-reproduction. The only hint of difference in McDonaldland involves Uncle O'Grimacey, an occasional (mid-March) visitor who speaks in an Irish brogue and is defined by his obsession with Shamrock Shakes. The emphasis is on standardization and "sameness"; all Ronald McDonalds go to school to make sure they conform to a uniform image. The training system is so rationalized that students are tracked throughout their preservice and in-service experiences into one of two groups: "greeting Ronalds" and "performing Ronalds." The most compelling manifestation of conformity in McDonaldland involves the portrayal of the French Fry Guys. As the only group of citizens depicted in the Hamburger Patch, these faceless commoners are numerous but seldom seen:

> They tend to look, act, and think pretty much alike. Parent French Fry Guys are indistinguishable from children and vice versa. They are so much alike that, so far, no individual French Fry Guy has emerged as a personality identifiable from the others. They resemble little mops with legs and eyes and speak in squeaky, high-pitched voices, usually in unison. They always move quickly, scurrying around in fits and starts, much like the birds one sees on sandy beaches. (McDonald's Customer Relations Center, 1994)

As inhabitants of a McDonaldized McWorld, the French Fry Guys are content to remove themselves from the public space, emerging only for brief and frenetic acts of standardized consumption—their only act of personal assertion.

Life in McDonaldland is hegemonically seamless and conflict-free; the Hamburger Patch is a privatized utopia. It is contemporary America writ small, corporate-directed and consumer-oriented. Issues such as distribution of income among classes, regulation of corporate interests, free trade, minimum wage, and collective bargaining once elicited passion and commitment—now they hardly raise an eyebrow. The political sphere, where decisions are made concerning who gets what and who voted for what, is managed by a small group. Their work and the issues they confront are followed by an ever-decreasing audience of news-watchers tuned to CNN and C-SPAN. Politics, Americans have concluded, is not only useless but—far worse in the mediascape—boring. It can't be too important: It gets such low

Neilsens. The political structure of McDonaldland reflects this larger depoliticization through its depiction of the inept and superfluous Mayor McCheese. The school promotional literature describes him as "silly," not "to be taken seriously." As a "confused and bumbling" politician, the mayor would rather spend his time in the privatized space of McDonald's eating cheeseburgers. The lesson for children emerges—politics doesn't matter, leave McDonald's alone, let these businessmen run their business as they see fit. The less individuals care about politics, the more effectively corporate hegemony can operate. Oppositional behavior is undermined before it can develop.

McDonaldland and Kroc/Ronald portray a benign capitalism free from serious conflict of any type. This picture is a cover for a far more savage reality. Business analysts such as Burger King's Jack Roshman, for example, liken McDonald's operations to the Marine Corps (Love, 1986). When a recruit graduates from basic training (Hamburger University), he believes that he can conquer anybody (ibid., p. 113). Motivated by an econo-tribal allegiance to the McFamily, store operators speak of faith in McDonald's as if it were a religion (Love, 1986). Kroc openly spoke of the Holy Trinity—McDonald's, family, and God in that order (1977, p. 124). On a mission for a theology of success, these faceless French Fry Guys have forced thousands of independent restaurant owners out of business (Luxenberg, 1985, p. 9). Competing fast food managers tell of encounters with recent Hamburger University graduates who promise to run them out of business and bury them in a hamburger graveyard (Love, 1986, p. 113). Inspiring such perspectives, Kroc was (in a way) the *Citizen Kane* of fast food.

No matter how ruthless business may become, there is no room for criticism or dissent in McDonaldland. "I feel sorry for people who have such a small and wretched view of the system that made this country great," Kroc wrote in his autobiography (1977, p. 180). The "academic snobs" who criticized McDonald's struck a sensitive nerve in Kroc's psyche and motivated counterattacks until the day he died. This love-it-or-leave-it anti-intellectualism finds its McDonaldland expression in the Professor. Described as a proud possessor of various degrees, the Professor is a bumbling fool with a high-pitched, effeminate voice. As none of his theories or inventions ever work, he meets Kroc's definition of an overeducated man: someone so preoccupied with inconsequential affairs that he is distracted from the normal problems of business. Kroc never liked books or school and saw little use for advanced degrees: "One thing I flatly refuse to give money to is the support of any college" (Kroc, 1977, p. 199). Intellectuals do not fit into the culture of the Hamburger Patch.

As much as the Professor is effeminate, Big Mac, McDonaldland's policeman, is manly. The promotional literature describes him as "the strong, silent type. His voice is deep and supermasculine; his manner is gruff but affectionate . . . his walk is a strut. His stance is chest out, stomach in." The gender curriculum of McDonaldland is explicit: Big Mac as the manly man; Birdie, the Early Bird, as the pert, nurturing female. As the only female in McDonaldland, Birdie is faced with a significant task. She is the cheerleader who encourages the male residents to jump into the activities of the new day. "Her enthusiasm and energy are infectious . . . her positive attitude is emphasized by her bright, perky, cheerful voice" (McDonald's Customer Relations Center, 1994). Once the McDonaldlanders have gobbled down their Egg McMuffins and are off to their respective occupations, Birdie retires to the sidelines as a passive observer.

Pissin' on Its Turf: Devouring the Competition and Hegemonizing the Sign

This masculine ethic runs through the corporate culture, expressing itself in a variety of ways. One sees it at work in McDonald's apparent obsession with *defeating* its competition. Millions of research dollars are dedicated to exploring and attempting to appropriate any cuisine or signifier that might prevent the sale of a Big Mac. When old-fashioned diners began to make a comeback, McDonald's designed and opened a Golden Arch Cafe and a couple of McDonald's Cafes, where customers place orders at the counters and are given stand-up number cards so that food can be delivered to their tables. In the early 1990s, when Burger King began to make inroads into McDonald's share of the market with its "Have it your way" advertising motif, McDonald's countered with "What you want is what you get." When Boston Chicken began to experience success in 1994, McDonald's launched Hearth Express, offering a variety of entrees and side dishes behind a glass counter. Just like Boston Chicken (later Boston Market), the McClone offered chicken, ham, and meatloaf with potatoes and corn on the side. We will bury you, McDonald's tells its competitors, even if we have to become you (Garfield, 1992; Whalen, 1994a).

This competitiveness spills over into the domain of signification, where McDonald's stands ready to do battle with anyone who messes with the company's sign value. So hegemonically powerful are corporate signifiers in the politics of the contemporary era that McDonald's spent tens of millions of dollars in the 1990s suing two unemployed British activists for tarnishing the McSignifier (Vidal, 1997). Disney legally forced a small group of New Zealand parents to remove images of Mickey Mouse painted on playground equipment, and Universal Studios established a telephone hotline to report unauthorized *Jurassic Park* images (Goldman and Papson, 1996). So successful is McDonald's at protecting and promoting the Golden Arches that the sign recently surpassed the Christian cross as the second-best-known signifier on earth. The *McDonald's-sponsored* Olympic rings are first (Vidal, 1997, p. 135). After $20 billion worth of promotion in the 1980s and 1990s, over 95 percent of American children recognize the Arches. In 1995 alone the company spent almost $2 billion on advertising outside the United States. Such economic power makes it difficult for even the most repressive state regimes to censor electronic messages from McDonald's (Kellner, 1998).

Despite its marketing successes and its colossal power worldwide, McDonald's corporate body still operates with the same thin skin that characterized Kroc. Incensed by criticism of the company, Kroc threw legendary tantrums in the boardroom (Kroc, 1977, p. 166). When critics blasted the quality of the food or the ethics of the organization, Kroc— intuitively understanding the ideological dimension of McDonald's sociocultural role—accused them of opposing the free enterprise system (ibid., p. 180). Shifting to a different language, Kroc did not want anyone to provide alternate dimensions to the McDonald's signifiers. He would have hated to see the struggles over the sign in the years following his death, expressed by new terms such as "McWorld" (the globalized, corporated commodity culture emerging in the 1980s and 1990s); "McJobs" (low-paid, low-status, dead-end work); "McGrub" (low-quality fast food); and "McUniversity" (low-quality, diploma-producing, impersonal, capital-driven higher education). All of these signifiers are connected to serious issues that face contemporary global societies: McDonald's and its contested signifiers stand at the cusp of history and the hegemonic factors that shape billions of lives around the world.

Even changes in the architectural style of McDonald's restaurants are saturated with signifiers with hegemonic dimensions. The McDonald's restaurants of the 1950s, with their white spaceship tile and neon lights and their science-fiction architectural angles, signified a post–World War II belief in the future, a suburban southern California-as-paradise optimism. With the sudden death of the New Frontier and the 1970s backlash against racial, gender, and sexual liberation movements and the Vietnam depression, McDonald's architecture turned nostalgic. As most of the early futuristic outlets disappeared, they were replaced by homelike wood and brick structures signifying comfort rather than ebullience. Such symbols hailed a hegemony of recovery, as they expressed a longing for an era of unchallenged WASP male dominance and the construction of family values. An imaginary icon of the McDonald's vision of America in the early 1980s might have depicted a Norman Rockwell version of the famous Edward Hopper diner, with Ronald Reagan eating a Big Mac under the Golden Arches.

The soft "recovery-of-what-we've-lost" ads of the era depicted family values in the suburban brick and wood McRestaurants to win hegemonic consent (Bell and Valentine, 1997, p. 134). Television commercials showed All-American "Parent Trap" children engineering meetings of their separated parents at McDonald's. Meanwhile, management were poised to pounce on anyone who interfered with the company's pristine signifiers, no matter how powerful or how weak. When Bernard Shapiro and Daniel Prather, for example, opened McDharma's, a vegetarian restaurant in Santa Cruz, California, they were served a court order to get rid of the "Mc" in its name. Even when

they painted the international symbol for forbidden—a circle with a diagonal slash—over the "Mc," McDonald's was
not satisfied and continued the suit. Nor was McDonald's
impressed by McDharma's counterhegemonic advertising:

> OVER 10,000 COWS SAVED!
> OVER 125,000 BURGERS SOLD!
> Dharma's Good for You
> Naturally Fast, Delicious Food
> Good for You
> Good for the World. (*People*, 1988, p. 81)

A few years after taking care of these vegetarians, executives went after sign usurper Mary Blair, who owned a
tiny sandwich shop in Buckinghamshire, England. Because
she was Scottish and liked the word "munchies," she
changed the name of her shop to "McMunchies." In September 1996 Ms. Blair received a letter from McDonald's
giving her two weeks to take down the sign and change the
name or face a lawsuit. Unable to fight the threat, Blair
complied, and the McMunchies threat to the sanctity of the
signifier was thwarted (Vidal, 1997, pp. 44–46).

When sign appropriation works in the opposite direction,
McDonald's employs a different strategy. By choosing the
name "Leaps and Bounds" for a chain of indoor playgrounds,
McDonald's usurped the name of a nonprofit church-affili-
ated educational program in Chicago that helped parents
teach their children learning skills through play. When the
name overlap was brought to the company's attention, legal
representatives informed the educational program's direc-
tors that McDonald's newly acquired federal trademark took
legal precedence over their Illinois state trademark. The program was left with no option but to change its name.
McDonald's has pursued similar signifier battles around the
world (Vidal, 1997, p. 45; *Advertising Age*, 1991).

Such competitive zeal is also reflected in the way McDonald's management views the company's future. Since less than one percent of the world's population visits McDonald's on a given day, executives proclaim in effect that the company has just begun to fight. We want to dominate every market in the world, CEOs maintain, as the company spends more and more money on winning the consent of the planet's inhabitants (Kovel, 1997). It is already the largest real estate owner in the world, having surpassed Sears in 1982. As the company bought roadside land outside city limits, it began to change the face of American towns and cities. Inducing other fast food companies and franchises from muffler and tire shops to hardware dealers to follow it, McDonald's unleashed a process that reorganized the relationship between central cities and their suburbs. The commercial centers of many towns perished, and with them city tax bases. McDonald's expansion is not, of course, the only cause of urban blight, but it has played an important role in it. Indeed, McDonald's is a central player in a multitude of forces that have changed North America and now the world (Monniger, 1988).

As prime roadside locations in the United States have become scarce, McDonald's has chosen to expand in alternative venues such as Wal-Marts and post offices. The prime location for McDonald's future, however, is definitely outside North America (Whelan, 1994a). In the modernist mind-set, quality is equated with size, and expansion is its own reward. McDonald's expansive mind-set supports a hegemonic logic that produces, in concert with other corporations' goals, dramatic social and cultural effects. As McDonald's power has changed the face of America, it has also helped change the minds of people around the planet. Understanding, for example, that the McLibel trial and the

McSpotlight website had alerted thousands of people to it's the impact of beef production on the Brazilian rainforest, McDonald's deployed its power to change hearts and minds. In Australia the company constructed a pseudo-rainforest at the Adelaide Zoo to demonstrate its commitment to environmental protection, accompanied by a wave of public statements about the fragility of these "environmental treasures" (McDonald's handout from Adelaide Zoo, 1999).

In handouts provided at the Adelaide Zoo and pseudo-rainforest, McDonald's waxed eloquent about its environmental concerns. We have developed an environmental management program that permeates all of our corporate operations, McDonald's told the Australians. Understanding the fragility of rainforests, McDonald's protects them by buying no beef from what was or is rainforest land. As all of its restaurants work to save water and energy, the corporation claims that it has become a world leader in environmentalism. In this role McDonald's Australia has constructed a Gorilla Forest and an Orangutan Rainforest Home at Taronga Park Zoo—exhibits, the company claims, that have raised standards for zoos worldwide. Other aspects of the company's environmental leadership, the literature tells readers, involve the Dolphin Research Institute and environmental and species preservation projects in Victoria (Adelaide Zoo handouts, 1999).

McDonald's Hegemonic Power to Shape Identity

Such pronouncements and the information control they represent help McDonald's construct the political consciousness. Of course not everyone believes the hype; different individuals will react differently to McDonald's positioning of itself as one of the world's strongest forces for environmental protection. Some people are radicalized by the perception of flagrant hypocrisy. But many will believe the claim, incorporating it into other positive corporate representations in a way that moves them to become defenders of the status quo, advocates of the neo-liberal effort to lower corporate taxes, create good business climates, and reduce requirements for corporate social responsibility. Why should society regulate corporate activity, they ask in the spirit of the free market, when companies like McDonald's are struggling to save our endangered rainforests? Thus, hegemonic power helps produce new political subjects, persons with a new respect for the tenets of the market and the needs of capital. Many interviewees with positive feelings toward McDonald's were angered by questions that addressed the issue of company duplicity. Their comments suggested an acceptance of a market truth: Whatever corporations needed to say to protect their product was validated by the imperatives of profit making.

Such a hegemonic truth (epistemology) works to commodify the individual, to produce what are called "disciplined subjects." Thus, the corporate control of information provides companies like McDonald's with a strong position in the subtle struggle to re-educate the world's peoples, to turn them into advocates of the unbridled free market. The corporate impact on identity formation is a cog in the larger hegemonic mechanism that commodifies, fragments, and injects images into the collective consciousness. A critical sociological imagination helps us understand the ways in which institutions like McDonald's shape the lives of individuals: The Frankfurt School of Critical Theory described this process in terms of the ties between the economic life of society and the psychological development of its individual members (Kellner, 1992). This complex and ambiguous dynamic is often missed by ethnographers and other researchers because its manifestations must always be interpreted. In interviews most people cannot clearly articulate the process by which a hegemonic logic has shaped their ways of seeing—especially in response to direct questions about how power in general or McDonald's power in particular has affected them.

McDonald's use of information to produce a rational process of consciousness construction is not unimportant, but an extremely significant aspect of the hegemonic process involves the way human needs and desires are colonized via an affective route. Here McDonald's produces a discourse and a set of signifiers that construct experiences and ways of perceiving and feeling that position the corporation and its ideological trappings in a positive light. In one conversation a young enlisted woman in the U.S. Army expressed the complexity of this hegemonic dynamic when she spoke rationally about the power of corporations but became profoundly agitated when a question raised the possibility of a hegemonic role for McDonald's in her own and her children's lives.

> I'm free to make my own decisions and no one needs to tell me I'm not. I love my country and the free enterprise system and my children love McDonald's. I know and they know that it exerts power but we're smart enough to know what to listen to and what to turn off. Everyone knows not to believe everything McDonald's advertisements tell us—no one falls for the political stuff. (Interview, 1998)

"If it is so irrelevant," I asked, "why do corporations like McDonald's keep spending so much money to promote the 'political stuff?'" She became angry at the question and at me.

> I don't understand why you are so obsessed with this. Can't you just accept the way this society operates? You can't be suspicious of everything. The people at McDonald's are just people like you and me.

The printed words do not convey the frustration and anger this young mother expressed. From a hermeneutic perspective I find these emotions quite significant. Is it ethnographically inappropriate to elicit such anger? Is it inappropriate to analyze its meaning as part of a discourse of hegemony? I certainly did not intend to anger the woman or any of the other interviewees who became angry. Indeed, it seems somewhat taboo in the ethnographic community to admit conflict with research subjects. But in the study of power and its effect on consciousness/identity/subjectivity, aren't difficult and potentially emotion-evoking questions necessary? The colonization of affect and desire is by definition an emotional topic. And dealing with that dynamic as a researcher, I would argue, will always be messy, ambiguous, disconcerting, and to some degree conflictual.

This does not mean that the researcher should set out to confront subjects or purposefully enrage them—not at all. The point is that research about power and subjectivity can never operate as smoothly and seamlessly as the mainstream ethnographic community might like. In the case of the young servicewoman, at no point did I attempt to anger her or show her disrespect. The subject matter, not the tone, of my questions made her uncomfortable. Her anger, I believe, was evoked by my implication that McDonald's hegemonic power may operate beyond the scope of one's conscious awareness—she interpreted that as an insult to her intelligence.

Cyborgs in Space: Hegemony and the Fabrication of Postmodern Identity

Consumption, whether of BMWs or Big Macs, is a cultural, economic, and political process in which issues of agency (self-direction) are constantly intersecting with forces of hegemony. The meanings of eating at McDonald's are inscribed by both desire and rationality and cannot be reduced to one or the other (Miles, 1998). As a society, Americans have not developed a language to discuss the notion that we visit McDonald's not simply to eat but to buy a way of living—an identity that ostensibly has little to do with milkshakes, fries, and burgers. Indeed, in a postmodern culture food is no longer simply about sustenance—as my parents saw it through the lenses of their Depression-scarred, Southern Appalachian identity. Able to generate strong emotions, food and the act of consuming it reflect and shape self-identity (Wyngard, 1998). The scene in Quentin Tarantino's *Pulp Fiction* where Jules (Samuel Jackson) and Vincent (John Travolta) discuss McDonald's in Europe is an example of how we understand our identities through food—in this case McDonald's food. The way the characters recoil at the Dutch custom of putting mayonnaise on French fries encodes them culturally as Americans with particular tastes, culinary boundaries, and societal identifications (Bell and Valentine, 1997, pp. 2–3).

The hitmen Jules and Vincent are transformed by their consumption-based knowledge of McDonald's into cultural brothers of American viewers. They share our culinary cultural capital via their McConsumption; they and we as viewers and fellow consumers gain social fulfillment as the consumers of both product and knowledge of the McDonald's brand. Even through Tarantino's screenplay, McDonald's power works to shape our identities, our understanding of our "selves." Identity formation via McDonald's consumption is strong enough to equal or, in specific situations, even surpass the identity-producing power of race, class, gender, religion, or sexuality. The fact that Jules is African American or that the two characters kill people for a living does not mitigate an American audience's identification with them via the commodity culture of McDonald's. Numerous science-fiction movies feature the creation of personal biographies—fabricated identities—for androids. McDonald's hegemonic production of identifications and identities presents us all with mediated experiences on which we draw for meaning in our lives. McDonald's and other corporate-produced "memories" make us all quasi-cyborgs (McCyborgs?) with minds in part assembled and animated by those institutions that control information (Goldman and Papson, 1996, p. 121).

Cyborgian subjectivity orbits the nucleus of what is known as the postmodern condition. This commodified self—in existence for roughly the last four decades—has never been stable but is constantly transmogrified by evershifting signifiers, from "you deserve a break today" to "the grown-up taste of the Arch Deluxe." Everyday life, while not unimportant, plays a lesser role in the production of identity as media representations take on greater importance. Thus, In the postmodern condition, McDonald's offers not only of *use* value through a commodity, food (a modernist notion), but, significantly, *identity* value through a set of hegemonic meanings. McSignifiers exist as a linguistic form that communicates ideas about ways of being throughout the world. Children and adults are integrated into the McDonald's discursive space by entering the restaurant or engaging with its advertisements. This integrative process of identity formation often conflicts with the socialization efforts of more traditional and (in the case of the religious right, for example) neo-traditional families and homogeneous communities. This is one of many reasons why traditional parents feel such a loss of control over their corporately integrated, consuming children. In my own life

I felt the same integrative gravity and witnessed the discomfort it caused my rural-community-identified parents. In this case and many others, McDonald's, even in a postmodern space, signifies a process of modernization (Deetz, 1993; du Gay et al., 1997, p. 91).

Hegemony and Disciplinary Power: McDonald's and the Signifier of Modernization

Disciplinary power is an important feature of the study of power. Simply defined, disciplinary power is an attempt to win hegemonic consent via strategies that produce notions of normality and abnormality in both the larger society and individual consciousness. People internalize such notions in a way that positions the "discipline" as natural and unconscious (Cooper, 1994). Examples of this disciplinary production of ab/normality include clinical psychology's delineation of sanity/insanity, the school's determination of smart and slow, or the fashion industry's assertion of beauty and ugliness, to name only a few. In this disciplinary context, McDonald's has used its capture of the signifier of modernity or modernization to distinguish the contemporary and up-to-date from the old-fashioned, outdated, and backwater. In the globalized society this disciplinary power plays out in a variety of modes and in diverse venues. Regardless of its locale, such power grants McDonald's even more access to the deepest recesses of human subjectivity and makes it a social force of tremendous weight. Best of all for McDonald's, such disciplinary power can be exerted with little notice.

When McDonald's opened a restaurant in Coudersport, Pennsylvania (population 3,200), in September 1996, the local paper celebrated the validation of modernization symbolized by the event.

The day it opened, it seemed all Potter County streamed in. "Now," said 15-year-old Matt Seeley, "we don't have to drive 40 miles for a Big Mac anymore."

On that day last September, two American institutions— one the stuff of tradition, the other the stuff of all-beef patties and sesame-seed buns—converged. On that day, McDonald's met Main Street.

Many citizens were ready for the McDonald's that opened on the edge of their downtown. It meant a spot on the map. It meant that they were plugged into the modern American goulash of advertising, commerce and popular culture.

Coudersport once faced the same fate as many of its neighbors: population drift, fading industry, a youth exodus.

But in the mid-1980s, entrepreneur John Regis' company, Adelphia Cable Communications, began growing rapidly. He kept its headquarters in Coudersport; Adelphia's increasing success brought a growing base of skilled labor to the region.

"McDonald's knows where to locate," Truppi says. "If they locate there, it's probably going to work. And that's a good indicator for this small town." (Anthony, 1997)

We have come of age, many Coudersportians exclaimed, finding civic and personal confirmation in their proximity to the fast food empire. What other commercial enterprise could have elicited such a response? Inscribed in those Golden Arches, emerging from the point where the southern California suburbs met the desert in the 1950s, is a vision of American modernity with all of the fast-paced, automobile-based, optimistic mobility that the *Zeitgeist* of that time and place could muster. The vision, tarnished and tattered by the social and cultural changes of the last half-century, remains sufficiently seductive to elicit attempts to recover it. While this recovery expresses itself in a variety of sociopolitical and cultural ways, one aspect still involves the power of McDonald's to validate the modernization efforts of villages like Coudersport. Jesse Jackson could have spoken for many of the residents as the Golden Arches went up: "We are somebody!"

If the *symbols* of "Westernness" and modernity converge under the yellow and red outlets, the signifiers also have *material* features. The McDonald's decor appears Western to those from outside the West; indeed, the way customers are addressed and managed is seen as very American. The organization and processing of its products are viewed around the non-Western world as markers of modernization, and so, as Ritzer (1993) correctly points out, is the rationalization of the entire McDonald's operation (Mintz, 1997). The failure of the Golden Arch Cafe in Hartsville, Tennessee, where a meatloaf lunch and other old-fashioned diner foods were served by traditionally attired waiters, taught the company an important lesson: McDonald's is not about traditional rural areas or small towns and the symbols of such places in the domain of food services. While McDonald's may raid such signifiers for patriotic and family values capital, its semiotic power hails a post–World War II American suburban modernity. No matter how small the town or how rural the market, McDonald's executives learned, customers want the restaurant's standard menu. In light of this knowledge, the company has retained the hegemonic power of the modernization signifier by constructing smaller "express" outlets in low-population areas (Solomon and Hume, 1991).

A Curriculum of Consumption

I have always been disturbed by the way McDonald's has targeted black people with ads like the one with Calvin getting the job at the restaurant. I have spoken with many of my friends about the way McDonald's is exploiting African Americans with such commercials and with the high-

cholesterol food particularly harmful to black folks. Nobody wants to listen to me. They tell me to "chill," because there's nothing we can do
about it. Politics doesn't work—it doesn't solve anything. (African American teacher in Louisiana, interview, 1989)

In its power to signify modernity and the inadequacy of the
precorporatized life, the McDonald's ideology teaches us
that the company is just too mighty to fight—so why not
just relax and get away? Join us, enter consumer heaven
through the Golden Arches. As the corporation has linked
this modernist utopia to culture and technology, it has
helped produce a new era of consumption. The corporate
ownership of television networks and other information-
producers and -transmitters has shaped a curriculum of consumption that has changed the lives and values of people
around the world—children and young people in particular—and made material ownership more important than
ever before.

Any capacity the media might have had to monitor the
unprecedented rise of corporate power has been squashed
by corporate ownership of the means of knowledge production. When McDonald's corporate partner, Disney, owns
ABC and McDonald's spends millions of dollars a year
advertising on the network, ABC's criticism of the Golden
Arches is going to be muted. ABC's and other U.S. networks' coverage of the McLibel trial, for example, was min-
imal. Corporations are profoundly affected by public
opinion; unbridled access to public airways allows them to
delineate political viewpoints in ways so subtle that many
individuals are unaware of the persuasion taking place.
While this process is complex and ambiguous and does not
always work in the ways McDonald's hopes, it nevertheless
operates well enough to justify the company's yearly multi-
million-dollar advertising expenditures.

The partisan political nature of McDonald's and other corporations often goes unrecognized by a populace "taught" to be naive about power. Never before have political entities possessed so great a capacity to shape opinion with so little opposition (Deetz, 1993). In this information environment and new culture of power, McDonald's operates to shape subjectivity at cultural micro-levels revolving around emotions and desires that many mainstream political analysts ignore. When the company connects individuals' passion for Beanie Babies to the McDonald's signifiers, an important process of micro-power inscription is occurring. When this process is combined with thousands of other corporations' micro-inscriptions, and all of these are subtly connected to macro-politics (ideologies, values, understandings of who produces pleasure, etc.), a new political era has emerged (Best and Kellner, 1991). In this new epoch television commercials and programming become the new educators, political philosophers, and historians. Indeed, we are pressured to believe that the "free flow" of information produced by television is the seminal fluid of contemporary democracy. And it does leave a nasty hegemonic stain.

McDonald's visibility and its willingness to use its political power in a variety of ways induce progressive political analysts to view the company as a social regulatory agent. In other words, the company emulates the disciplinary tasks of schools, mental hospitals, cognitive psychology and its testing industry, and theme parks (Gottdiener, 1995). In this regulatory context, progressives trace McDonald's techniques of bringing together ideological, hegemonic, pedagogical, and disciplinary forms of power. From this perspective, McDonald's represents the quintessential corporate power-wielder and identity-shaper of twenty-first-century globalized society. It is not surprising that McSpotlight and anti-McDonald's campaigns around the globe have elicited such strong emotional support. This reaction draws upon a growing disdain in particular locations for global corporate activity and the austere, capital-friendly, neo-liberal state policies that support it.

Rich Texts, the Richness of Social Construction, and Rich Fudge Sundaes

McDonald's reflects modernist macro-power structures and hyperrationalism in organizational form (as Ritzer [1993] states) while operating in a culturally driven, globalized, information-saturated, postmodern cosmos. The juxtaposition of the modernist and postmodernist is can lead to misinterpretation, and analysts who attempt to read the McPhenomenon as simply one or the other miss the complexity of the process. A key to McDonald's sociocultural, political, economic, and educational role is an understanding of the conceptual border where its modern and postmodern characteristics intersect. Understanding this may help us appreciate the complexity of power, domination, and the production of political subjectivity in the first decade of the twenty-first century. One reason for the gulf between cultural analysts and contemporary citizens is the critical intellectuals' inability to find a language to communicate this complex modern–postmodern cultural dynamic and its implications for life in democratic societies. A discursively/socially constructed, mediated (media-filtered) reality clashes with the public's nostalgic desire for an easily discernible sociopolitical universe. Thus, we search for a simple language to describe a complex reality.

The public expresses its desire for uncomplicated knowability in the call for unbiased news reporting, a depoliticized school curriculum, nonideological political behavior from elected officials, and easy moral choices. The same desire can be uncovered in the faith that a burger is just a burger. People who believe this operate in an epistemological dimension where nothing exists between absolute objectivity and total relativism. A public that does not understand the nuances of social construction does not possess the conceptual tools to assess the complex ways in which the political dimension operates in globalized, mediated society. I am not contending that the public is unable to understand such dynamics—indeed, people are quite capable of such insights. Given the ways in which information and political knowledge are produced in contemporary society, however, a corporate-driven cultural pedagogy teaches people not to appreciate the complex social construction of consciousness, the power dynamics involved in the production of one's point of view.

The richness of McDonald's as text never ceases to amaze. A cursory delineation of generative codes would include: heroic entrepreneurship, unbridled capitalism as sacred faith, family values, efficiency as moral value, cleanliness as a marker of high civilization, conventionality as a position in the cultural war, entertainment as social regulation, value (as in "value meal") as a form of economic democratization, and consumption as an exalted expression of humanness. As these codes intersect with global capitalism and the ideology of free enterprise economics, new mutations of culture and cultural pedagogy are animated, producing bizarre subjectivities lacking grounding in sophisticated analytic or interpretive abilities. Individuals often have not acquired the conceptual tools to choose between competing interpretations of cultural artifacts. A conservative publication like *Reader's Digest* can comfortably claim that the "Mc" in McDonald's "has come to mean something akin to big," as in "McBucks" (Ola and D'Aulaire, 1988, p.

40). In the progressive periodical *The Nation*, a cover story in March 1998 on the triumph of the market in Chile was signified by a picture of the Golden Arches—a sign for exploitative, globalized market capitalism. The cultural wars raging at the ideological poles are illustrated by these diverse readings of the McDonald's text. Yet most of the public is unable to make sense of the entire politicosemiotic process.

Agents of Hopelessness: Despair in the Midst of the Boom

It is not uncommon to uncover descriptions of McDonald's "as the most visible symbol of the global economy" (e.g., Wilken, 1995, p. 6). Observing McDonald's in Turkey, Brazil, and Fiji and the company's impact on local culture, one can understand the Golden Arches as a reminder of the dramatic success of capitalism's global commodification. In this global context, the process of knowledge production is commodified and used to further the needs of corporate clients to gain further power. Because of the inherent instability of global postmodernity, this process of commodified knowledge production must increase if corporations are to keep up with the constantly changing cultural and semiotic temper. Without such information McDonald's would not be able to alter the ways it represents itself to different parts of the world. This transformation of the corporate sphere and the world's interlinked economies is a central aspect of the contemporary McDonald's story. The company's relationship to and attempts to deal with these new realities provide insight into both McDonald's and the socioeconomic changes themselves (Alfino, 1998; Smart, 1992).

McDonald's understands itself as a global entity, aware that its future is centered outside rather than inside the United States. As a global employer with more workers than the entire U.S. steel industry, McDonald's sees itself as ungovernable in terms of any traditional notion of public governability. In the new global order, McDonald's is one of the many Big Bad Wolves of transnational corporations that huff and puff and threaten any state that attempts to mold their actions. McDonald's and other multinational firms account for two-thirds of world trade—about a trillion and one-half dollars a year and rising. McDonald's huge work force is, of course, disadvantaged by the managerial power the firm wields. Despite pronouncements by Presidents Clinton and W. Bush and many others about the rosy future of the U.S. economy, McDonald's workers have come to represent the status of many contemporary American laborers. The economic boom of the late 1990s was reserved for the middle and upper classes, as the United States became the largest low-wage economy in the world. Most male workers, for example, now earn less in real dollars than they did in 1973 (Martin and Schumann, 1997).

This decline in wages is accompanied by a concurrent elimination of production skills through rationalized and standardized procedures. For ever-increasing numbers of workers, this trend simplifies jobs or gets rid of them and the workers who perform them. McDonald's crew positions, the McJobs, have come to signify the new types of jobs replacing the ones people have lost. Even in the retail and catering business, McDonald's jobs pay in the bottom quartile, have 120 to 150 percent turnover rates, are marked by consistent managerial violations of employment regulations, keep workers in a "frantic" state of mind, and demand overtime work for no extra pay (Kovel, 1997, p. 29). Even Judge Rodger Bell, who presided over the mismatched McLibel trial, ruled that McDonald's pays its employees such low wages that it helps depress wages for all workers in the catering trade in Britain. Compared with other retail outlets, McDonald's offers starting pay lower than the average for similar work (McLibel Newsletter, 1997). Since young people make up a large percentage of McDonald's employees, the Golden Arches have come to be viewed as an important contributor to lower-middle-class youths' hopelessness around the world: Indeed, McDonald's low-paid, low-skill jobs with few opportunities for advancement have contributed to working-class young people's loss of faith in the modernist story of hard work and mobility (Giroux, 1996).

It is easy to understand their apathy and powerlessness and appreciate the etymology of what their elders read as a "bad attitude." Having put in their time at the McJob, how can they escape the alienating effects of managerial and corporate disdain? As David Rikert's management case study on McDonald's puts it: "I think managing is the ability to manipulate what you have" (1980, p. 7). Reading Rikert's case study, which is used in business schools, I uncovered little embarrassment at using the language of manipulation as long as it was enfolded in the lofty rhetoric of the company's striving for pride and excellence. Indeed, McDonald's has to gift-wrap its management strategies because, until the restaurants are fully automated, workers (as in all service industries) will still be needed. McDonald's is more vulnerable to worker organization than is the manufacturing sector—a domain where labor can be controlled by threats of corporate migration to Malaysia. This is why McDonald's managers around the world have often fired workers engaging in union activity (Kovel, 1997). They are painfully aware of their company's exposed flank.

In the McLibel trial, for example, McDonald's managers admitted that they would fire anyone engaging in union activity in British outlets (Kovel, 1997). All around the world, McDonald's has fought unionization using state-of-the-art tactics. Operating with a huge antiunion war chest, the company has been known to bring in 15 lawyers to fight organizational efforts in one restaurant (Featherstone, 1998). In poor countries like Indonesia, where McDonald's workers earn 57 cents an hour (below the legal minimum there), the corporation does not hesitate to threaten union members and fire union leaders (Featherstone, 1999). In Moscow unionized workers are barred from talking to one another during work hours and frequently watch helplessly as their 40-hour work weeks are cut in half (ibid.). Observing such global trends, it seems safe to maintain that McDonald's unions rarely prosper in places with numerous poor people such as Indonesia, Russia, Mexico, and parts of the United States. Indeed, in this country McDonald's harsh labor policies and ideological influence contribute to downward mobility, a decline in the public sector that traditionally provided some protection for the poor, and an economic system biased against less skilled workers (Russell Sage Foundation, 1999).

I Do Not See the Elephant in My Bed: Turning the Global into the Local

It is hard to view McDonald's relationship to labor or corporate power outside the context of globalization. Everything about the company is connected in some way to the global context. Indeed, as a key player in global technocapitalism, McDonald's is hard at work restructuring world markets to support the maximum accumulation of profit. Yet both George Ritzer and John Watson seem unable to grasp the significance of this globalization process as it relates to McDonald's sociopolitical role in the new planetary order.

Ritzer (1993, 1996), in his disdain for anything postmodern, ignores the company's globalization dynamic, while the authors of *Golden Arches East* (Watson, 1997) are unable to grasp the relationship between and the inseparability of globalization and localization. McDonald's has globalized its production and marketing operations while providing an opening for local readings and idiosyncratic cultural appeal. It is producing a global culture—but not a homogenized one. The McWorld is mediated through local conditions and local perceptions. A successful hegemonic force would operate no other way (Goldman and Papson, 1996, p. 124; Kellner, 1998; Kellner, forthcoming).

McDonald's has worked meticulously to set up "local" operations headquarters in diverse locations with high-visibility "corporation men" to run them—Den Fujita in Japan is a notable example. The corporation has mastered the global–local nexus, developing localized products for local consumption (Bastable, 1993):

"Oriental" chicken salad
Fried chicken
Teriyaki burgers
Banana fruit pies
Halal burgers—made with beef prepared in accordance with Muslim dictates
Durian milkshakes—made from a fruit that tastes like a sweet onion
Kiwi burgers doused in beetroot sauce
The McLak—a salmon burger
French fries with chili sauce

This localization within globalization is consciously promoted by McMarketers via a personalization motif. "You deserve a break today" has been transmogrified into "*My*

McDonald's." These restaurants claim the ultimate local status—they're *yours*, whether you are from Beijing, Fiji, Tel
Aviv, or Peoria. And this, curiously, is what anthropologist
Watson does not get: McDonald's customers are induced to
produce idiosyncratic meanings of the Big Mac. When their
customers "customize" the meanings of their consumption,
McDonald's marketers have succeeded. Watson reads this
marketing/hegemonic success as a marker of resistance to
overblown critical conceptions of transnational corporate
power. As reviewer Samuel Collins (1998) summarizes the
argument of Watson et al.: "Consumers are shown to exert
a sort of plucky, subterranean control over otherwise mono-
lithic corporations." In the same conceptual context, Collins
quotes James Cantalupo, president of McDonald's International, and offers his own comments:

> The goal of McDonald's is to "become as much a part of the
> local culture as possible." He objects when "people call us a
> multinational. I like to call us a *multilocal*, meaning that
> McDonald's goes to great lengths to find local suppliers and
> local partners whenever new branches are opened." I [Collins]
> would suggest that multinationals, far from advocating homo-
> geneous "global cultures," are comfortable with a notion of
> culture similar to Hanes Watson's "local culture." (Collins,
> 1998)

So eager is McDonald's to implant this perception of
localization/personalization in the public mind that the company actually employs a vice-president for individuality
whose stated function is to make "the company feel small"
despite the reality of globalization (Salva-Ramirez,
1995–96). In Beijing McDonald's markets itself to the Chinese people not as an American company, but as a Chinese
one. Executives invest time and money in publicizing the
restaurants' local features, including the local production of

the beef and potatoes. The vast majority of the staff members, they are quick to assert, are Chinese. Like the other contributors to *Golden Arches East*, Sangmee Bak (1997) misses the point. Despite omnipresent and fierce debates about Americanization and transnational corporate exploitation in Korea (Collins, 1998), Bak falls back on Watson's comforting thesis that Korean customers of McDonald's use creative consumption to transmutate the restaurants into Korean institutions. When researchers focus simply on the process of consumption and omit any reference to production—in this case McDonald's marketing strategies—it is not surprising that power is erased. A complex, power-driven global–local process is magically transformed into a happy individualized game of creative consumption.

A central feature of George Ritzer's argument in his *McDonaldization of Society* (1993) involves the assertion that McDonald's is rendering the world homogeneous and systematically subverting diversity. While there are undoubtedly homogenizing influences at work, the impact of McDonald's is far more complex and its influence is heterogeneous and variegated. Overgeneralizing the homogenization thesis, Ritzer left himself open to the criticisms of Watson et al. and their ethnographic documentation of diverse receptions by East Asian consumers.

Ritzer erred in relying on an anachronistic deployment of the expose of the anti-individualistic features of "mass society" provided by the Frankfurt School of Critical Theory. Critical theory put forth its mass society conformity thesis in the 1920s and 1930s. Since at least the 1970s, critical analysts have recognized the limitations and reductionism of the early massification thesis. Contemporary critical theorists are well aware of the plethora of ways in which individuals in diverse locations receive the meanings and signifiers of the Golden Arches (Kellner, 1989; Kellner, 1998; Kincheloe, 1995; Kincheloe and Steinberg, 1997).

Watson and his collaborators are focused so closely on countering Ritzer's allegations of cultural homogenization that they shield McDonald's leadership from complicity in environmental problems, growing childhood obesity in East Asia, economic exploitation, labor abuse, gender inequality, and other impacts (Collins, 1998). And despite Ritzer's and Watson's observations about cultural homogenization, as far as corporate leaders are concerned, consumers' multiple readings work in concert with managers' desire to enhance profits. If McDonald's is attempting to become an integral part of the local culture, the company is, according to Watson, succeeding. Indeed, it is so successful that it has diverted attention away from the social sins broadcast by McSpotlight and the McLibel Support Campaign (Bak, 1997; Yan, 1997).

Interweaving the Modern and the Postmodern

The literature on McDonald's illustrates the operation of the constructivist axiom that one's theoretical perspective shapes what one sees in the world—the present author not excluded. When observers bring a postmodern lens to their research, they can easily observe the way McDonald's produces knowledge in order to optimize the efficiency of its organizational performance. We have observed this dynamic in McDonald's representations of itself and its products in ways that win consent for its profit-making. Operating from a Weberian position, Ritzer observed McDonald's and saw a new stage of capitalism and an enhanced, speeded-up version of technical innovation and rationalization. An important hermeneutical point needs to be made here: Modernist and postmodernist aspects of McDonald's are not in conflict with one another. We can interpret McDonald's simultaneously as a modernist and a postmodernist phenomenon, and binary, either/or positions miss the power synergy between McDonald's modernist rationalization of production and consumption and its postmodernist deployment of signifiers in the contemporary electronic, globalized culture.

The phenomenal success of the McDonald's corporation is not possible without both components. As the restaurant operates with a rationalized efficiency that produces standardized products, its advertisements connect this dehumanizing process to the pseudo-personalization of the colonization of affect (Kellner, forthcoming; Martin and Schumann, 1997; Smart, 1992). In this way individual desire is tied to the sign of the Golden Arches—a sign that goes far beyond food. Indeed, a central aspect of the modern/postmodern synthesis involves inscribing features of modernization with local culture to make it appear unthreatening to the consumer. Thus, in the Tennessee of my youth, McDonald's modernization process was mitigated for more traditional, premodern consumers with restaurant murals celebrating University of Tennessee football—a sacred icon of the local faith. For me and countless Appalachian contemporaries seeking to shake off our traditionalism, the modernization signifier became an end in itself—we needed no mitigating cultural cushions.

Thus, we weave modern and postmodern insights in the pursuit of what Steven Best and Doug Kellner (1991) label a multiperspectivist analysis. As previously argued, the richness of the McDonald's text, derived in part from its location between the modern and the postmodern grants it the kinetic power to shed unique light on the most compelling issues of our era. For all the limitations of Ritzer's Weberian analysis, his concept of McDonaldization helps explain a variety of processes taking place in many locales. Through Ritzer's eyes we are able to trace an important macro-dynamic at work around the world. Rationalization and its McDonaldization variant attempt to produce intractable mechanisms to deal with messy, often irrational, ever-changing situations. One sees this process constantly at work, unfortunately, in contemporary schooling, cognitive psychology, and formal research, to name only a few domains. Such forms of systemization are out of step with the complex phenomena they address and thus distort human situations in a manner that often leads to regulation (Wa Mwachofi, 1998).

Ritzer's critique of McDonald's rationality is obviously important, but from our perspective, concerned about the effects of the culture of power and domination, it is unsatisfactory. Rationality at McDonald's, like its manifestation in other domains, is important because of its material effects. McDonald's rationalization helps the corporation regulate individuals and shape their consciousness in order to enhance its power and profit. If Watson dismisses the existence of the political economy, Ritzer never seems to connect rationalization to this realm. Without such a connection, readers are left without insight into the most basic feature of McDonald's contemporary operation—its effect on material culture and individual human beings. A critical deployment of postmodern analysis, especially as it relates to the colonization of culture and the use of affect to produce consciousness, could help rather than hinder Ritzer's attempt to understand McDonald's material effects.

Efforts in this work to study the semiotic and language-related features of McDonald's have not moved us away from the analysis of the culture of power and its material effects. On the contrary—they have enhanced our understanding of how globalized corporate power operates. Understanding these textual aspects of McDonald's helps us grasp the ways in which hegemonic meanings are mobilized and relations of domination are initiated and sustained. Indeed, our *critical* textual analysis of McDonald's illustrates how semiotic/discursive dynamics shape individuals' perceptions of the restaurant *and themselves in relation to it*, and then hide the manner in which this dramatic task was accomplished. Until this bizarre feature of power in hyperreality is exposed, the public will find it difficult to gain a critical political consciousness. These dynamics help us explicate the ways in which power is working in the first decade of the twenty-first century to change the world; they show us the connections between the manner in which meaning is constructed and the ways it supports social regulation and domination. With these insights we can track the relationships between discourse and structure. Viewed in the context of the McDonald's corporation, we can see how its self-representations and social inscriptions are connected to the structures of globalized capital (Alfino, 1998; Aronowitz and DiFazio, 1994, p. 175; Kellner, 1998; Thompson, 1987).

Interpreting Reception: The Trouble with Consumption

In discussing the interpretive richness of McDonald's as a text, it is important to focus on the relationship between the production of meaning and the consumption of meaning. Production and consumption are obviously linked, but questions and debates arise when analysts attempt to describe the nature of the relationship. McDonald's consumers are certainly not passive victims who view the company simply as it represents itself. They sometimes resist and reject

McDonald's-generated meanings and often use productions in ways that the company did not intend. In the hermeneutical dance between McDonald's and its customers, marketers work to motivate consumer behavior that increases McDonald's profitability and power while consumers have various interests. Watson and colleagues, I have argued, focused too much attention on the consumption aspect of the dyad. Yet the subjectivity of reception is certainly important. Consider these insights from an Egyptian interviewee, describing his movement to a more "ironic" view of McDonalds (similar to my own shift, described in Chapter 1):

> After arriving in the U.S. and gaining a familiarity with McDonald's in this country, I began to reflect upon the role that the company had played in my life. I began to see the ways the marketing in the U.S. was designed to suck in people just like me. I look back home to Egypt and friends tell me how McDonald's and places like it are emphasizing the differences between those that can afford it and those who can't. Places like McDonald's may cause a civil war in countries like mine. I see McDonald's in a very different way than I did when I was younger. I can do without my Big Mac. (Interview, 1996)

More traditional sociological studies were often concerned exclusively with production. In the traditional paradigm, the process of production of a consumer item *determined* the meaning received by those who used it. A study like Watson's *Golden Arches East* can be viewed on one level as a postmodern overreaction to this disciplinary tendency. Here I want to examine the relationship between production and consumption of meanings about McDonald's in a way that avoids essentialism. Unlike Watson, I believe that the production process is a necessary aspect of the meaning-making process; at the same time, production always interacts with consumption and the particularities of the context in which they take place. Thus, while the meanings—both intended and unintended—produced by McDonald's are always important, they are not universal or forever determined. Signifiers change as the *Zeitgeist* changes. Thus, a burger is never simply a burger, and what it means today may change tomorrow.

Because of the idiosyncrasy of reception, therefore, McDonald's does not produce a neat and tidy hegemonized individual. Yet, although cultures and individuals are not homogenized, the company's power-saturated discourses and ideologies certainly shape the public's sociopolitical perceptions. There is nothing very complex about this assertion; people perpetually mediate their sociocultural and economic experiences via positions in the world related to race, class, gender, sexuality, religion, geographic place, and countless other dynamics. Such positioning shapes the ways in which McDonald's signifiers and products are employed in an individual's life and consciousness construction.

At this point critical researchers encounter profound epistemological problems, for there is no way an analyst of McDonald's can empirically "prove" a cause–effect relationship between McDonald's production of meaning and individual political consciousness. Because this empirical link is so hard to establish, McDonald's and other corporations are consistently denied to have ideological influence. During the question and answer session following a speech I gave on McDonald's, an audience member challenged me to prove my interpretation of McDonald's cultural and political role. I responded that such proof, such empirical certainty, is unobtainable in a hermeneutic process like cultural analysis. The questioner, unimpressed, asserted that my work was mere opinion. I agreed with him that, like all interpretations, it was "mere opinion," but I hoped it was a compelling opinion. These are the conversations that emerge when paradigms collide.

Indeed, "the impact of McDonald's" and "ways of receiving ideology" are such complex concepts that new research methods must be devised to analyze them. Since the audience/receivers of McDonald's messages are not present at their production, they cannot be studied in the way traditional ethnography has approached its subjects. Receivers exist in a different space from producers, a territory in hyperreality shaped by particular social, cultural, and political-economic circumstances. This interrelationship between production, contextual circumstance, and reception is always complex and ambiguous. Focusing on any one piece of the puzzle without the others will lead to reductionism and distortion. The ideological/hegemonic and discursive meanings produced by McDonald's never completely control consumers. This is why the company pays marketers, advertising agencies, and designers so much money: to monitor reception and keep reconfiguring meaning production in order to address consumers' changing perceptions and changing social circumstances. McDonald's must constantly work to legitimate itself within an information environment littered with signifiers and ideological messages. Sensing challenges to its representations both unintended (the exhaustion of a particular representation, resulting in receiver indifference) and intended (McSpotlight), McDonald's works harder and harder to bolster its sociopolitical and semiotic position (du Gay et al., 1997; Schiller, 1993; Thompson, 1987).

Thus, consumers of McDonald's products and messages do not have an interpretive "blank check"; their consciousness is not a virginal *tabula rasa*. What McDonald's means is

shaped by power at the level of production, social circumstance, and reception. Who has the economic power to
finance the production of messages? What are the forces
that shape dominant ideologies, discursive practices, political economies, information environments, and other social
circumstances? How are subjectivities, identities, and con-
sciousnesses constructed in ways that affect the reception
process? These are central but often ignored questions in the
analysis of the consumptive act in general and the reception
of McDonald's meanings in particular. They are all directly
about the workings of power. In the complex contemporary
culture of power, meaning is not simply connected to statements reflecting a "communication community" but is
inseparable from the discourses, ideologies, and signifiers
produced by deep structures of domination. How individuals make sense of McDonald's messages cannot be isolated
from the deep political-economic structure associated with
the sanctity of free enterprise and the "entrepreneur makes
good" ideal.

Here sociological and cultural studies analysis leaps onto
a more rugged terrain. The intersubjective meaning-making
of McDonald's consumers/receivers is not simply a personal
matter of individualized perception; it is also a process
shaped by world views and competing interests. Corporations like McDonald's have more power than any other
group in the world to shape the information individuals
encounter. This threat to the delicate democratic balance of
power becomes more and more pronounced as analysts
realize that corporate hegemony can be used to produce
human needs. In the case of McDonald's, such needs may
not be in the consumer's best interests (unhealthy food), but
may be in the producer's (big profits). While the meanings
of McDonald's cannot be simplistically universalized, the

reality of domination and power cannot be ignored. As corporate power has increased over the last 25 years, time for family, civic participation, and leisure has decreased. Corporations have used their power to cultivate a consumer lifestyle made possible by an increased commitment to work and a forfeiture of self-directed time. These material changes, unlike many effects of corporate power, are measurable. Such a material change seems improbable without concurrent modifications of consciousness.

As a producer of power and burgers, McDonald's taunts social analysts to make sense of its effects. In the case of the company's interaction with children and young people, our need to understand the meanings in operation and their effects on consciousness is practical and important. The connection between children/youth and consumption/reception of corporate representations is gaining significant attention, as studies point to the escalating consumption demands of "Generation Y" (Neuborne, 1999). In a child-unfriendly era (see Steinberg and Kincheloe, 1997), McDonald's and other marketers understand that consumption provides youth with a sense of empowerment. Such a sensation is intoxicating in a world of danger, isolation, and dismissal and can shape values in a dramatic fashion. Young people may exchange a sense of uniqueness for the pleasure, community, and reassuring meaning they find in consumptive practices. A McDonald's burger, therefore, is not simply a food product but may be a pacifier in a world of uncertainty. Such an insight provides a hermeneutic window through which we can begin to see the affective investments individuals (ourselves included) make in their consumption of McDonald's hamburgers and other products (Deetz, 1993; Gottdiener, 1995; Kellner, 1998; Miles, 1998; Mumby, 1989).

Interpretive Experiments in Hyperreality:
McDonald's as Religious Ritual

In an era when advertising and information production
work to break down traditional belief systems, public
expressions of scientific rationality, and the grand narratives (such as religious traditions) by which people shape
their lives, social analysts must develop a variety of interpretive schemas. Such modes of social analysis produce
ways of examining postmodern phenomena such as the
sociopolitical impact of power agents like McDonald's.
Employing the frame of social ritual—in this case religious
ritual—gives us another angle on McDonald's ability to
make meaning and shape consciousness. Applied to the
McDonald's phenomenon, this conceptual framing illumi-
nates aspects of the cultural process hidden in the informational chaos. Viewed as part of a larger religious ritual,
consumption of McDonald's food and representations
becomes more than simply an individual act. In this context
one is better able to discern the relationship between meaning production and reception, between demographically significant collective activity and idiosyncratic behavior.

In the context of McDonald's as religious ritual, the secular and sacred begin to merge, as low-culture McDonald's
plays a more sacred role in the everyday life of hyperreality.
Without the grounding of unquestioned grand narratives,
the lived significance of McDonald's exceeds previous expectations. "McDonald's can't be that important to you," parents admonish their McDonaldized (in the cultural sense)
children. The parents do not realize the power generated by
McDonald's ability to engage their children in its public ritual. The company itself cannot refrain from using phrases
like "we're father, minister, and rabbi" to the hordes of

young people engaged in its on-the-job training (Vidal, 1997, p. 38). Such ritualization is certainly in the company's interest, for the more ceremonial consumption becomes, the more likely consumers are to engage in it. Watching Americans frequent McDonald's outlets in Germany, Holland, and France, one quickly understands how comfortable they are with the ritual. A sense of familiarity engulfs American tourists as they enter the restaurants and—like Tarantino's Jules and Vincent—compare German, Dutch, and French names for familiar McDonald's products.

Thus, McDonald's in a cultural context becomes a holy ground; the mundane, via the power of information control and signification, transmogrifies into the consecrated. In some restaurants McDonald's promotes the hallowed signifier, employing stained glass and architectural styles more reminiscent of a low-rent basilica than a "hamburger stand." The late 1990s "My McDonald's" ad campaign suggested a comparison: my McDonald's occupies a role similar to "my church." The financial writer Penny Moser (1994) innocently expresses the concept:

> A new one has replaced my old McDonald's in Aurora, Illinois. The manager said old faithful just got tired and sagged in 1981. My new hometown McDonald's, in Washington, D.C., is much different. I have to wend my way through the street people to reach it. But when I get there my friend Felipe, a Salvadoran refugee born with only one arm, will serve me with a smile. He wants to go to Hamburger University someday and become a manager. After that he'd like to own a franchise. (p. 116)

A disconcerting identification with McDonald's and sense of ownership materialize in this passage. David Wu (1997) contends that in Taiwan, McDonald's now occupies the role of "social magnet" once played by temples, to which people would come not only for religious purposes, but to socialize, gossip, and conduct business. It is not surprising, therefore, that Wu concludes that the Golden Arches hold a deeper symbolic meaning for contemporary Taiwanese children than does the traditional temple.

This religious dynamic was never lost on Kroc, who always saw the company in theological terms. To survey where the Golden Arches might expand, Kroc would lease planes to help him spot church steeples. Wherever suburban churches were located, he reasoned, McDonald's customers were lurking (Love, 1986, p. 164). The same conventional values that moved them to attend church would induce them to eat at McDonald's. Kroc intuitively understood his target audience and the semiotic similarities between the Golden Arches and the Cross; somehow he discerned the kinetic sacredness of his entrepreneurial creation. With the breakdown of traditional narratives of rationality in hyperreality, McDonald's religious aspect manifests itself in bizarre ways. In various Big Mac TV commercials over the last 25 years, the sandwich, like God on the Sistine Chapel ceiling, gives life to inanimate objects. McDonald's can heal the sick, raise the dead, and make the little children go out of their heads.

In this Trinitarian theology, Kroc is God the Father, Ronald the Son, and the McCorporate vision the Holy Spirit. Company executives "celebrate" Kroc's birthday, the McChristmas, by working in holy sublimation in an outlet, mopping floors and cleaning toilets—In His Service. In a corporate act of transubstantiation, the blood in believers' veins turns to ketchup, signifying their rebirth into the McFamily. Such believers in the company's executive ranks refer to themselves as Kroc's apostles (see, e.g., the profile of Robert Beavers in *Black Enterprise* [1988], subtitled "The Apostle of the Golden Arches"). Executives and other believers who make the pilgrimage to the company's suburban Chicago headquarters can engage in McPrayer at the "Talk to Ray" exhibit. Visitors can phone Kroc the Father and hear him speak on a variety of subjects, recorded on tape before his death (Salva-Ramirez, 1995–96). After their encounters pilgrims often testify about their experiences with McDonald's. They bear witness to their first hamburger or describe their hometown McDonald's:

> After that first meal in 1957, McDonald's never left my life. Although my family moved about northern Illinois, we were never far from Mac's. I remember the whole family, with Grandma or an uncle in tow, remarking when the sign under Speedee's running legs changes . . . 100 million sold . . . 200 . . . 300 . . . 500. (Moser, 1994, p. 115)

The affective investment individuals, myself included, are making here far exceeds any rational, simplistic, cause–effect explanation. McDonald's crosses the border separating the realm of material consumption from the sanctification of the secular. In my 1998 talk radio appearances, numerous callers justified this sanctification process by referring to Kroc's and McDonald's "good works"—the "social gospel" of the Golden Arches. "What about the Ronald McDonald Houses?" radio callers implored. "They do a lot of good. What about McDonald's concern for and contributions to local communities? Nobody supports sports like McDonald's." It took billions of dollars to build such reverence—no one ever said doing the Lord's work was cheap. As managerial communicants read and study their McBibles—Kroc's *Operations Manual*—they become enthralled by the emotional pull of the McFamily and the specificity of the holy scriptures' instructions. At the Seminary (Hamburger University), managers learn in addition to highly specific cooking instructions what shades of fingernail polish are permissible (Salva-Ramirez, 1995–96).

Thus, the McDonald's religion—Krockism—is a fundamentalist theology that reveres the letter of the law. Its formula for success (salvation) is not open to interpretation—there is no need for McDonald's hermeneuts. The job of the Seminarians is to go back to their outlets and proselytize about burgers, special sauce, success, and the free enterprise system. Once again, the ideational aspects of the Seminary's curriculum and the corporate theology are just as important as the burgers themselves. In this context the burger is made word—a miracle in the McDonald's faith. As Kroc posthumously presides over the burger empire, the clown manifestation of Kroc on earth, Ronald McDonald, rules as titular head of the company's terrestrial semiotic structures. In McDonaldland cartoons and comics, Ronald consistently "saves" past, present, and future residents by bringing them the *grace* of the burger.

If the Golden Arches are more recognizable in the world than the Christian cross, Ronald is second only to Santa Claus in recognizability by children. Kroc was obsessed with Ronald's image and personality—he even determined the design of his wig. Ronald was created to bring the children to McDonald's and was intended to accomplish the task in the same way any sacred figure would: by winning their love. Understanding the importance of his vicar in the symbolic cosmos, Kroc, like the Jesuits, knew that if Ronald got kids before they were five years old, McDonald's would have them for life. As Geoffrey Giuliano, a former Ronald McDonald, recently confided, working as the holy clown is "very much like a religious cult" (McSpotlight, 1997). So profound are the theological semiotics of McDonald's and Ronald the Son that religious relics—like the pieces of the "true cross" sold in the Middle Ages—have begun to turn up in cyberspace. The *Antique Appeal* ran this ad in September 1996:

RONALD MCDONALD HEAD FOR SALE

—two foot Ronald McDonald head dated 1977
—used to blow up balloons in restaurants/play-grounds
—good condition
—asking $195

6 The Struggle for the Sign of the Burger

In the story of McDonald's, one can trace many of the important historical changes of the last 50 years. McDonald's initial success reflected the mobile, car-centered, increasingly fast-paced life of economically prosperous post–World War II America and children's expanding impact on consumption decisions. The restaurant's growing success in the 1960s reflected women's entry into the outside-the-home work force—it was quite convenient for working mothers to stop by McDonald's on their way home from work to feed the family. In the last quarter of the twentieth century, McDonald's success pointed to the reality of overworked Americans with little time to cook. Its movement around the world over the last couple of decades displays the emergence of the globalized economy and the cultural changes that have accompanied it.

Living and Dying in Hyperreality:
McDonald's Cultural Contingency

Despite the fast-paced and alienated culture we all face, McDonald's with all its convenience is there for us—"You deserve a break today." The slogan does not have to designate what the break is from. We already know—it is a break from the stress of hyperreality, the postmodern condition.

185

Before hyperreality businesses only had to produce goods and services—consumption took care of itself. McDonald's and other corporations have come to understand that in the new postmodern social order, consumers and their desire for particular products must be produced. Not only is this process more costly than the production of goods and services, it is also more subtle and exacting. The production of consumer subjectivity and desire must move beyond some simple, direct appeal to the individual; it must rearrange larger social structures and cultural forms. Thus, McDonald's does not just sell hamburgers to individuals; it also sells lifestyles and affective dispositions that position McDonald's consumption in a larger psychosocial matrix.

Countercultural orientations such as those connected to Greenpeace and the values and lifestyles of Dave Morris and Helen Steel are dangerous to McDonald's because consumption at the Golden Arches falls outside the realm of the "acceptable" in such ways of being human. Thus, McLibel is not merely about corporate criticism but about forms of life in contemporary global society. Dave and Helen struck at the very soul of McDonald's sociological countenance and cultural meanings. Corporate marketers count on the confusion of hyperreality to render consumers culturally perplexed. When consumers are in a hermeneutic free fall, they are set up for advertisers poised to insert corporate consumption values into the vacuum left by the dissolution of previous beliefs. Almost nothing serves the marketer's agenda better than the decline of various communities and their shared values. In this sociocultural context, new market values and pseudo-celebrations of "traditional values" (now rearticulated and connected to the Golden Arches) can perform ideological, discursive, and hegemonic tasks (Deetz, 1993; Luke, 1991).

In this new cultural cosmos, consumers struggle to make meaning. The conflicting dynamics at work in hyperreality push and pull them in different directions, putting them both in sync with and in opposition to corporate marketing interests. McDonald's, with its power to produce information, counts on its ability to manufacture new traditions via common experiences and shared expectations: We all know that McDonald's song, Ronald McDonald, the taste of a Big Mac, the ritual of the drive-through, and the rest. We have all watched children beg for McDonald's food; those of us of a certain age observed the counting ritual as the marquee tally of burgers sold changed from 24 to 25 billion. McDonald's creates narratives like these to provide us with a sense of identity—one that is positively connected to McDonald's, the ideology of free enterprise, and the semiotics of Americana. The forms of community and social relations that are absent from our lives in hyperreality but present in our desires are reinscribed around the Golden Arches by the McDonald's ads. Any organization capable of tapping into such deep-seated features of our psyche possesses an unprecedented form of power.

As contemporary market capitalism removes the social safety nets established from the 1930s through the 1960s and public expenditures for families and communities decline, McDonald's presents itself as the force to fill the vacuum. Why should we worry about the poor when we have McDonald's as a cost-effective haven open to all? Why should we worry about sick children when we have Ronald McDonald Houses? Why should we worry about lonely children when we have the McDonaldland characters? Why should we worry about children having parks to play in when we have McPlaygrounds at the outlets? Why should we protect the environment when we have McDonald's

Rainforests? Why should we expend monies on public spaces when McDonald's is underwriting everything from the Olympics to public schools? The ideological constructs McDonald's produces cause citizens to ask such questions. In the process the traditional definitions of "the public" and "the private" are reconfigured, and the boundaries between them are blurred. Thus, the New Corporate Order marches on, reinscribing everything in its path (Goldman and Papson, 1996; Kovel, 1997).

But the process of reinscription is never easy. Hyperreality is a mean place where corporations and other organizations can live or die. Representations and signifiers change meanings as time passes—especially in the saturated information environment of the beginning of the twenty-first century. Yesterday's "hip" signifiers will be embarrassing tomorrow. If McDonald's does not keep evaluating and updating its semiotic dimension, its image may become the seventies leisure suit of fast food. In the late 1990s, despite its power and success, McDonald's came to be viewed by some market analysts and journalists as that leisure suit, anachronistic and out of touch with cultural changes (Manning and Cullum-Swan, 1998). Although the company's early history was by no means free of conflict, charges of being out of touch were new for the McManagement. As McDonald's has come to understand in the first decade of the twenty-first century, living and dying in hyperreality means engaging in a never-ending semiotic war over corporate signs. As company executives dealt with charges that the Golden Arches were out of touch, they faced new modes of attack on their signifiers. The postmodern irony of David Letterman represents a semiotic subversion, as he parodies the rhetoric of media discourse. While Letterman's salvos alert a few (at most) to the hegemonic and ideological dimensions of the culture of power, they disrupt the semiotic intent of McDonald's self-representations and force McMarketers to intensify their efforts to control their sign values.

Facing a string of failed products and promotions and a public relations debacle in the McLibel trial, executives bristled at Letterman's references to marketing bombs such as the 55 campaign and the Arch Deluxe (both described below). Letterman was not the only one to parody McDonald's signifier problems in this period. Sensing the vulnerability of the Golden Arches, KFC ran television commercials featuring a Ronald McDonald–like character testifying before a congressional committee. The stumbling and sweating clown was depicted as unable to answer interrogators' questions about the nutritional value of McDonald's food. The ad symbolized well the public perception of the company. The attack was based on its marketing failures, not ideology or principles, for KFC had as much to lose in that domain as McDonald's. Rather, it was a critique from *within* the free market, an attack on McDonald's loss of the ability to protect its image.

Falling Arches: Semiotic Troubles at Century's End

As management worried over damage to its sign value, it expanded the company's promotional efforts. In the summer of 1995, McDonald's connected the firm's image to three cultural artifacts at once. Creating promotions around the movies *Batman Forever* and *Power Rangers* and the 1996 Atlanta Olympics, the company bombarded customers with popular signifiers. As sometimes happens in hyperreality, the multiple sign connections confused customers. Sales increases fell far short of projections and competing fast food movie tie-ins. At the same time, Burger King, for example, produced significant sales increases with its *Pocahontas* deal. Once again, McDonald's suffered a semiotic marketing failure. After long and successful lives, their signs were beginning to die in hyperreality (Benezra, 1995).

Business writers began to take a different approach to the Golden Arches. Once the signifiers began to fray, such journalists wrote of challenging times for the fast food giant, aggressive competition within the fast food sector, changing American tastes, and saturated markets (Hamilton, 1997). Many of the articles suggested that American society was evolving past the appeal of McDonald's. As Martha Hamilton (1997) wrote in the *Washington Post*: "The colossus of the drive-through landscape has watched the ground beneath the Golden Arches begin to erode, at least in the United States" (p. H1). For the first time in burger history, McDonald's "same store" sales declined while Burger King's and Wendy's were up. This was due in part to McDonald's own success—so many outlets had been built in the previous 15 years that the market was saturated. Nevertheless, the McDonald's signifier was facing a different reception, a cultural change that undermined its stability.

This crisis of signification forced McDonald's to act. After serving as CEO for 11 years, Michael Quinlan was pushed out and replaced by domestic operations chief Jack Greenberg—the fourth CEO in the corporation's history. One industry analyst wrote that the beleaguered Quinlan had "presided over the demise of one of the great brands in the history of American business" (Damon Brundage, quoted in Marks, 1998). The change marked an important shift in McDonald's traditional hiring policy and relationship to the social and cultural world surrounding it. Kroc, as noted in Chapter 3, had been obsessed with employing executives who had started out on the lowly grill of one of the company's outlets. Both of his immediate successors, Fred Turner and Quinlan, had. At the end of the century, however, many felt that the firm's executive staff was long on practical experience and short on macro-economic, political, and social insight. The anti-intellectualism, the Kroc-cultivated shallowness, was taking its toll (Cohen, 1999).

Such criticisms were not coming from scholars in critical sociology and cultural studies, but from Wall Street analysts. Under this pressure, McDonald's broke with Krockism. Greenberg's appointment was McDonald's Vatican II. He came to the McFamily as chief financial officer in 1982, without having cut his teeth on the hamburger grill. He was promoted to chief of domestic operations in July 1997 and assumed the chief executive position in August 1998. Holding a law degree from DePaul University, Greenberg brought a nuanced view of international economics that many believe will become required knowledge for McDonald's upper management in the future (Kramer, 1997; "McDonald's Replaces Its Chief Executive," 1998).

Because he symbolized an important change in the corporate culture, McDonald's PR department repackaged Greenberg. To forestall criticism that he is not one of the guys, publicity was quick to announce that, despite his background, Greenberg has ketchup in his veins. Indeed, in an interesting and symbolic move one of the first changes the corporation made after his appointment to chair of domestic operations was altering the taste of its ketchup. Such changes are "spun" by McDonald's publicity as the work of a grand innovator and all-around-good-guy (Kramer, 1997). The corporation's representation of the new CEO comes across rather clearly in newspaper articles:

Carlos Roldan, 27-year-old manager of a New York City
McDonald's restaurant, looked up from his work one day last
July and saw Jack Greenberg walking in the door. Greenberg,
head of McDonald's Corp.'s U.S. business, was about to
become chief executive of the world's largest restaurant company. It was no perfunctory walk-through, Roldan recalls.
Greenberg presented him with a special McDonald's lapel pin,
mingled with employees and asked detailed questions about a
critical new made-to-order food system Roldan's restaurant
was among the first to adopt.

A month later, Greenberg—now officially chief executive—
was back, checking on the progress of the new system and
once again encouraging the troops. "He got involved," said
Roldan, who doesn't remember meeting Greenberg's predeces-
sor, Michael Quinlan. "We were very excited." (Cohen, 1999)

The Party has acted; the historical revisionism process is
now under way. Quinlan is out; Greenberg is in. Greenberg
is said to connect well with people, to elicit personal feelings
from his managers—he is "emotionally available." At the
beginning of the new century, Greenberg assumed the public role of the Bill Clinton of burgers, feeling the pain of his
executives and franchisees. Quinlan's last four years as CEO
had been profoundly painful and stressful. He oversaw and
assumed responsibility for one marketing and PR failure
after another, attempting to guard the castle while barbar-
ians of all stripes stormed the gate. The four years from
1994 to 1998 stand as McDonald's Dark Ages.

To irritate McDonald's and emphasize the Golden Arches'
market troubles, the barbarian Burger King built a large
restaurant near McDonald's Oak Brook headquarters outside Chicago. As CEO Quinlan eyed the encroaching Burger
King, he spoke of the "state of hostility" facing his company. The Golden Arches had completely dominated the
children's fast food market in 1985 (Hume, 1990). By the

mid-1990s numerous other companies had challenged their dominance, learning from McDonald's hegemonic ability to colonize children's consciousness. The phenomenal marketing success of previous decades, which had tied McDonald's semiotically to Americana and all the values that mainstream America held dear, was the root of the PR problems of the mid-1990s. Because the McSignifier was so well established in Americans' consciousness, any drop in sales or marketing disappointment was a surprise, a failure to meet traditional expectations. And in the media climate of the American TV landscape, surprises are what make news: McDonald's failures, not its successes, are "newsworthy."

Such an information climate tends to exaggerate corporate failures. McDonald's is without question still powerful, even if the image of the Arches has been tarnished a little. Overseas sales continue to grow dramatically, indicating the power of the signifier outside the advanced hyperreality in the United States. Similar marketing dynamics may occur in foreign markets when signifier saturation and postmodern cynicism reach present U.S. levels. Who knows? In the context of our concerns with ideology, representation, and hegemonic cultural pedagogy, power-wielders produce more information and values and shape consciousness and identity more effectively than ever. The curriculum of consumption is alive and working. The more corporations adopt the semiotic and affective formulas that worked for McDonald's and others, the greater their impact on who we are and what we believe as a society. The "falling arches" of the preceding heading refer only to one company's experience on the contemporary marketing battlefield in relation to its competitors. The larger struggle to deploy the culture of power to make political-economic meaning proceeds without interruption (Feder, 1997; Hamilton, 1997).

A cartoon by Fred Schrier in the *Washington Post* well illustrated McDonald's end-of-century position in the fast food industry. Cornered in an alley, a falling Ronald McDonald is beaten senseless by Colonel Sanders of Kentucky Fried Chicken fame, Wendy, and Burger King's crowned hamburger (Hamilton, 1997). As Colonel Sanders slugs Ronald, Wendy and the Burger King hamburger kick him in the head. When CEO Quinlan observed similar phenomena in the real world, he lamented McDonald's inability to counter such negativity with an exciting new product—in his words the company's "inability to hit a home run" (Horovitz, 1998a). Asked to explain the failure, Quinlan cited the research division's inability to gauge what Americans want. Asked the same question, fast food analysts speak of American consumers' changing tastes (Hamilton, 1997). McDonald's research department was well aware of these changing dynamics in the 1980s and 1990s: Increasing numbers of households with both husbands and wives working outside the home, more meals eaten outside the home, a larger number of people who wanted more variety and higher quality. And, the research insisted, they were willing to pay more. From these data emerged McDonald's adult-oriented, upscaled Arch Deluxe campaign. Unfortunately for McDonald's, the campaign failed (Hamilton, 1997).

Chairman Quinlan was not one simply to blame company failures on others. Research may have made mistakes, but the chair accepted his own contribution to the firm's millennial troubles. His biggest mistake, he contended, involved pushing for too many new restaurants in the eighties and nineties in the domestic U.S. market. Quinlan maintained that under CEO Greenberg's leadership, McDonald's would continue to expand in the American market but far more cautiously (Horovitz, 1998a). Despite the media's

"Where have you gone, Ray Kroc?" perspective, at the end of his CEO tenure Quinlan could point to record corporate earnings in fiscal year 1998. Moreover, according to the Interbrand Group (a consulting firm based in London and New York), the McDonald's brand/signifier passed Coca-Cola in the late 1990s to become the world's most powerful corporate name (Feder, 1997)—no simple feat in the cut-throat global business cosmos. Despite such displays of power, however, McDonald's executives were devastated by the reports (mentioned above) that during the wildly successful Beanie Baby promotion some customers dumped the food and kept the toy. Even though McDonald's had secured 240 million of the critters to make sure that their stock would not run out—almost a quarter of a billion babies—outlets still ran out occasionally, infuriating customers turned away empty-handed after waiting in long lines. From Quinlan's beleaguered perspective, the company had once again snatched PR failure from the jaws of success (Feder, 1997).

Perceiving challenges to the McSignifier all around it, the company kept searching for Quinlan's elusive "home run." After six straight quarters of same-store sales declines, marketers devised a price discount initiative in 1997. Recalling 1955, the year Kroc bought the franchise from the McDonald brothers, the campaign attempted to tie the optimism of postwar 1950s California to the changing conditions of the late 1990s. Big Macs would cost 55 cents, customers would be reminded of the company's meaning in its early days, and McDonald's would regain its momentum (Horovitz, 1998b).

Television ads displayed nostalgic black and white shots of the early walk-in/take-out restaurants, with their space age analogues and rocketship white tiles. Remember who we are and what we mean in your lives, the ads beseeched viewers. But the signifiers were not working in the way advertisers intended. In the late spring of 1997, hyperreality was draining the signs of their emotion and affect. After only six weeks of promotion, Campaign 55, as it was labeled, was killed. Franchisees had also opposed it, since the promotion offered free sandwich vouchers to any customer who did not receive a Big Mac within 55 seconds of placing an order. Underpaid and harried employees were livid about the time-compression stress Campaign 55 imposed. Their opposition revealed the tip of a growing iceberg of dissent among owners and managers. The U.S. expansion had so damaged owners of older outlets that McDonald's was forced to compensate them financially to keep the peace. Marketing failures begot a cycle of internal organizational problems (Horovitz, 1998a; Kirk, 1997; Kovel, 1997).

Signs of the Times: The Arch Deluxe Fiasco and the Importance of the Children's Market

Quinlan and his executives walked like Sammy Sosa, Barry Bonds, and Mark McGuire as they unveiled their long-sought "home run" food item in 1996: the Arch Deluxe. After two years of research and design dedicated to fashioning an upscale sandwich for adult tastes, the Arch Deluxe was hailed as the most important product launch in McDonald's history. Gourmet American cheese, transubstantiated ketchup, gloppy Dijon sauce (a mixture of mayonnaise and Dijon and stone-ground mustards), and iceberg lettuce on a "bakery-style" bun (as opposed to a non-bakery-style bun?)—the Arch Deluxe took its place beside the Big Mac and the Egg McMuffin. Within weeks it was obvious that the home run was a pop fly to the pitcher. Sales were low (Hamilton, 1997).

As a product designed for "adult tastes," the Arch Deluxe represented a significant shift in corporate strategy. Some observers have described it as signaling McDonald's move into a post-Fordist economic arrangement (Amad, 1996), a description that may require some explanation. The twentieth-century American economy has been described as a Fordist construct, a reference to Henry Ford's famous compromise. Ford raised salaries at his automobile plant to avoid worker–management conflict and simultaneously increase consumption and demand. In return for an opportunity to consume more, American labor tacitly agreed to tolerate meaningless and boring factory jobs. The Fordist compromise began to come apart in the 1970s with the oil crisis and the rise of foreign manufacturing in a globalizing economy. As observers debated whether or not a new economic era had begun, many described the new impulse as post-Fordism.

In post-Fordist corporate arrangements, marketers recognize that consumer interest in mass-produced products is being replaced by more concern with specialized items. Post-Fordist economic wisdom contends that contemporary consumers are becoming more and more attracted to quality and are willing to pay for it. Post-Fordist marketers spend much more time on social research and analysis of cultural dynamics in an effort to identify "niche markets" and target particular products to different "demographic groups." McDonald's analysts believed that they had identified such a group—aging baby boomers who had grown up eating McDonald's burgers but whose tastes had evolved with their increasing salaries. Thus, in a classic post-Fordist move, Quinlan and his executives deployed the Arch Deluxe as an effort to up-market the Golden Arches and tap the $5 billion-a-year gourmet burger market (*The Economist*, 1996). As

Chef Andrew Selvaggio describes the sensuality of the Arch Deluxe's seafood cousin, the Fish Filet Deluxe, it is obvious that he is not addressing McDonald's traditional clientele:

> The Fish Filet Deluxe has a complex build. First, I want your tongue to get a crispy seafood flavor from the pollock fillet coated with premium Japanese bread crumbs. Then, as you bite down, you sink into the welcoming crown of the potato roll, the creamy dill remoulade, a bit of flavor from the chopped onions. Then the cool contrast of crispness from leaf lettuce, the rich, melted American cheese and a little pepper note as a surprise. (Quoted in Parker, 1998, p. 1)

This Fordist/post-Fordist dynamic brings us back to our conversation about interpretation and the frames of modernism and postmodernism. George Ritzer's modernist interpretation of McDonald's—and his concept of McDonaldization in particular—emphasizes the corporation's Fordist elements. The McDonaldization phenomenon dovetails quite well with Fordism's cookie-cutter products, rigid technologies, standardized work routines, deskilling, and homogenization of workers and customers—important features of everyday life at McDonald's. But just as modernist and postmodern impulses co-exist in twenty-first century globalizing society, Fordist and post-Fordist modes of production operate in the same social space. In McDonald's both impulses can be simultaneously observed.

McDonald's post-Fordist assault on the upwardly mobile adult gourmet burger market not only abandoned its core clientele but actually *vilified* them. Adults may have participated in the popularity of the Beanie Baby giveaways and the McDonald's—Disney promotions around the movies *101 Dalmatians, Hercules,* and *George of the Jungle,* but these campaigns were first and foremost directed at children. Indeed, as we have noted throughout this work, the burger was not the main draw for the restaurant; it was the burger experience for children, who would drag their parents with them to the Golden Arches (Hamilton, 1997). When the company built playgrounds, conceived the Happy Meal, gave birth to Ronald McDonald and his McDonaldland entourage of consumer junkies, it was bowing to the desires of this core audience. In *Kinderculture: The Corporate Construction of Childhood* (1997), Shirley Steinberg and I trace the advertising tactics McDonald's has traditionally used to tap into children's desires and connect them to the Golden Arches. Viewed in light of the company's advertising history, the Arch Deluxe campaign is bizarre and disconcerting.

In connection with its family values signifier and its attempt to convince American parents that the company was concerned with the best interests of children, McDonald's marketing strategies always catered to the child. Kroc well understood that McDonald's public image should be, as he put it, an amalgamation of the "YMCA, Girl Scouts, and Sunday School" (quoted in Boas and Chain, 1976, p. 97). In the midst of social upheaval and instability, the Golden Arches endure as a rock of ages, a moral refuge for children in a world gone mad. McDonald's was "all about the children." The way the Golden Arches were "about children" took on interesting twists even during the height of McDonald's Family Values campaigns.

Ads of this era were devised to tap into a Reaganesque vision of the traditional family under attack from feminists, homosexuals, and other Kroc-defined "screwballs" (Goldman, 1992). In an ad produced in the early 1980s, a "typical" white middle-class family is visiting the small town of Dad's childhood. Eager to show his preteen son and daughter his childhood world, Dad tells the family that his old house is just up the street. As the "Greek chorus" sings,

"Things have changed a bit since you've been around" in the background, Dad is shocked to discover that new condominiums have replaced the old house. Dismayed but undaunted, Dad tells the family that his old friend Shorty's house is just around the corner. Shorty's house is also gone, replaced by a car wash. From the backseat the daughter tells her disappointed father that she hopes the place where he used to eat is still standing, because she is hungry. Dad immediately begins to look for the unnamed eating place as the chorus sings: "In the night, the welcome sight of an old friend." The camera focuses on Dad as his eyes brighten and a smile explodes across his face. Camera cuts to car pulling into McDonald's. The chorus sings: "Feels so right here tonight at McDonald's *again*."

As the family enters McDonald's, the message is implanted that consumption at the Golden Arches brings the family together and affirms the well-being of the children in a larger society marred by misguided left-wing do-gooders who threaten them. Nothing has changed here; Dad tells the perky young counter girl that he had his first Big Mac at this McDonald's. The camera focuses across the dining room to a short man expressing surprise and disbelief. Of course, it is Shorty. As Shorty embraces Dad, we find out that Dad's childhood name was Curly—ironic now, since he is bald. The camera retreats to frame the old friends embracing in the light cast by the Golden Arches. Dad is at McDonald's; he is home with old friends and family. McDonald's made it all possible (Goldman, 1992). The turbulent sixties are finally over. We (America) have "come home" to protect our children by readopting the traditional family values that made us great. The chorus has already reminded us that it "feels so right . . . at McDonald's again." We're going back, McDonald's assures us, to that more child-friendly time in the white, suburban, pre–Watts riots southern California world of 1955. We are returning to the "California Dreaming" and "California Girls" of the American paradise before it turned into a South Central, Rodney King, post-apocalyptic hell.

One of the interesting twists I refer to above occurs in the last scene of the "Home Again" commercial. The camera shoots a close-up of the son and daughter. Having just watched Dad and Shorty embrace, the daughter turns to her brother and says, with an ironic inflection, "Curly?" Her brother shrugs and rolls his eyes in recognition of the generational rift between Dad's understanding of the scene and their own. The reunion is irrelevant to the son and daughter, the camera tells us, as it focuses on the children's preoccupation with the hamburgers in front of them—the only time, by the way, McDonald's food is displayed in the ad. McDonald's wants it both ways: the adults' identification with the return to traditional family values, and the children's identification with a subversive kinderculture. This subversive subtext can be identified in a number of McDonald's advertising productions—especially in family-values-oriented ones. In the "Home Again" commercial it involves the children's shared recognition of the father's (Curly's) silly pursuit of a long-dead past and his embarrassing public display of emotion. Dad blows his "cool pose." Dad's/Curly's less-than-hip performance at the restaurant is the signifier for deeper generational divisions—differentiations described by advertisers as market segments.

Traditionally overlooked by marketers, children aged five to 12 spend almost $5 billion of their own money a year and influence household spending of almost $140 billion, more than half of which goes for food and drinks. Every month 19 out of 20 children aged six to 11 visit a fast food outlet. In a typical McDonald's promotion where toys such as Teenie

Beanie Babies, Hot Wheels, or Barbies accompany kids' meals, company officials can expect to sell at least 30 million meals to child customers. By the time they reach age three, over 80 percent of children know that McDonald's sells hamburgers. Indeed, McDonald's has worked feverishly to connect children to the Golden Arches (Fischer et al., 1991; Giroux, 1994; Hume, 1993; Ritzer, 1993).

Recognition of the covert kinderculture has played a significant role in McDonald's advertising over the last two decades. Understanding it and colonizing it gives McDonald's a unique pipeline to children's consciousness. The great irony of ads like "Home Again" is the fact that, under the flag of traditional family values, they actually undermine the family values they claim to promote. The McDonald's experience depicted does not involve a family sharing a common experience; instead, each market segment experiences it in a different and even potentially conflicting way. Curly's family, like so many American middle-class families, is an isolated unit divided against itself. In terms of everyday life, McDonald's does not encourage long, leisurely, interactive family meals. The seats and tables are designed to be uncomfortable enough that customers will eat quickly and leave (Ritzer, 1993). In the larger scheme of things, family values, America, and home are marketing tools designed to legitimate McDonald's to different market segments. Kroc made his own feelings about family very clear. Work comes first, he told his managers. "My total commitment to business had long since been established in my home." And Kroc commonly referred to the elements of the Holy McTrinity—McDonald's, family, and God—in that order (Kroc, 1977, p. 89).

One of the most important aspects of the company's semiotic troubles in the 1990s involved the McMarketers' new positioning of children. The "Home Again" ad hails the children, not Curly and the other adults, as the savvy ones. Child viewers quickly recognized and were charmed by this feature of the texts. Adults were not in the know; they were outside the club of the enlightened, perpetually represented as confused in these child-centered ads. McDonald's marketers recognized early on that the romantic representation of children as beings in need of constant adult protection and as naive innocents who should watch only "good" television was perceived by kids themselves as oppressive. Indeed, children at the beginning of the new millennium are not passive and naive television viewers. As advertising professionals working for McDonald's (and more and more other companies) have learned, children are active, analytical viewers who often make their own meanings of both commercials and the products they sell. These social and psychological dynamics between advertiser and child deserve more analysis.

By drawing upon children's discomfort with middle-class protectionism and the accompanying attempt to "adjust" them to a "developmentally appropriate" norm, advertisers hit upon a marketing bonanza. If we address kids as kids— with a dash of anarchism and a pinch of hyperactivity—they will love our commercials even though parents (especially middle-class parents) will hate them. By the end of the 1960s, commercial children's television and advertising were grounded on this premise. Such video throws off restraint, discipline, and old views that children should be seen but not heard. Everything, for example, that educational television embraces—earnestness, the child as an incomplete adult, the child as in need of correction—commercial television rejects. In effect, commercial television sets up a children's oppositional culture, a subversive kinderculture.

One does not have to look far (try any middle-class home) to find that children's enthusiasm for certain television shows, toys, and foods isolates them from their parents. Drawing on this isolation, children turn it into a form of power—they finally know something that Dad does not. How many dads or moms understand the relationship between Mayor McCheese and the French Fry Guys? Battle lines are drawn between children and parents as kids clamor to purchase McDonald's hamburgers or action toys. Conflicts in lower-middle-class homes may revolve around family finances; strife in upper-middle-class homes may focus on aesthetic or ideological concerns. Questions of taste, cultural capital, or self-improvement permeate child–adult interactions in such families. "You know you don't want those horrible hamburgers from McDonald's," middle-class parents attempt to persuade their children, often to little avail. In the video *Raw* comedian Eddie Murphy plays with the humor of these conflicts when he describes the difference between a homemade hamburger and one from McDonald's. Murphy's child character runs crying from his playmates as they make fun of his mama's hamburgers and gloat over their superior McDonald's burgers.

The child's ability to negotiate the restrictions of adult values is central to the development of an independent self. A very common aspect of this development of independence involves the experience of contradiction with the adult world. In the context of this childhood struggle for independence, a covert children's culture has developed. In the last hundred years, such a culture has existed on playgrounds and in schools. Before hyperreality, it was produced by children themselves and propagated through child-to-child contact. The postmodern children's culture of today is created by adults and dispersed via television for the purpose of inducing children to consume. As they carefully subvert middle-class parenting's obsession with achievement, play as a serious enterprise, and self-improvement-oriented "quality time," advertisers connect children's culture to their products. McDonald's commercials reflect these themes, although more subtly and adeptly than many children's advertisers.

Walking a tightrope between the wish to tap the power of children's subversive culture and the fear of offending the middle-class guardians of propriety, McDonald's has developed a core of "slice of life" children's ads depicting a group of preteens engaged in "authentic" conversations around a McDonald's table covered with burgers, fries, and shakes. Using children's slang to describe toys in various McDonald's promotions("radical, dude, we're into Barbie"; Seiter, 1993, p. 132), children discuss the travails of childhood with one another. In many commercials children make adults the butt of their jokes or share jokes that adults don't get (ibid.; Goldman, 1992, pp. 98–99). Subtly, McDonald's attempts to draw some of the power of children's subversive culture on to its products without anyone's noticing but the kids. Such slice-of-life ads are opaque to the degree that adults watching them do not see the ad's effort to connect McDonald's with the subversive kinderculture.

The Arch Deluxe campaign of 1996 continued this theme of intergenerational conflict but in a different form and with profound consequences. Ronald McDonald was "yuppiefied." Clad in a tuxedo and depicted as a social-climbing golfer, Ronald was not "just for kids any more." The adult–child conflict that had worked so well when handled *covertly* was now *overtly* displayed in the new Arch Deluxe commercials. McDonald's marketers positioned the gourmet sandwich as a rite of passage to postmodern adulthood. Depictions of angry African American children on billboards reminded adults that

kids viewed the Arch Deluxe as the Arch Enemy. More san-
guine-looking white children compared the adult sandwich to
spinach, cauliflower, and other banes of childhood. In these
ads intergenerational conflict was pulled out of the closet in
the same way that child abandonment was "outed" in the
Home Alone movies and packaged as "good, clean fun."

The children depicted in the Arch Deluxe ads are kids as
seen through adult eyes; previous ads captured children's
hearts and minds by depicting adults as seen by children.
The upwardly mobile Arch Deluxe niche market, McDonald's marketers assumed, viewed children with suspicion.
Indeed, in such a context kids, with their demands on time
and energy, get in the way. They are impediments to the
mobile, corporatized *dolce vita*, inconsistent with the
requirements of the time-compressed, dynamically flexible
post-Fordist cosmos. The ads position children in a way that
reminds both adults and children of kids' unfortunate
propensity for bad taste. The Arch Deluxe itself and the ad
campaign for it were produced as part of an overt effort to
capture the multi-billion-dollar yuppie market—a demographic segment in which McDonald's performs poorly. At
$2.29 ($2.59 with bacon) the Arch Deluxe was priced higher
than other menu items in an effort to add a snob appeal that
the company had carefully avoided for five decades.

In hyperreality the line between childhood and adulthood seems to be blurring, as children gain access to the
once-secret knowledge of adults via the media and adults
attempt to hang on to their childhood by any means necessary. McDonald's corporate soulmate Disney also sought to
lure an adult clientele in the period. Indeed, Frontierland
and Happy Meals are not just for kids any more. The failed
Arch Deluxe—the burger with the grown-up taste—was
merely an early manifestation of a cultural trend that many

predict will find expression in a variety of venues in the twenty-first century (Whitney-Smith, 2001). As the writing about the Arch Deluxe appeared on the wall, McDonald's executives confided that they had learned their lesson and would never again segment their market that way. As one executive put it: "We're making a very serious recommitment to the fact that the great thing about McDonalds is that the thought of it, or the experience, brings out the kid in everybody" (Hamilton, 1997, p. H6). The McMarketers claimed to be going back to basics, back to the signifiers that helped them gain their enormous power in the first place.

Confusion in McDonaldland: Returning to Basic Krockism or Forward to Greenberg's Post-Fordism

There was something inconsistent about these announcements. The contradictions were more clearly exposed after Greenberg's coronation in the summer of 1998 and his public statements about the corporate changes he planned to initiate. More than Quinlan or other upper-level executives, Greenberg was wedded to a post-Fordist vision of McDonald's future. He was a major architect of McDonald's problematic rapid expansion in the first six or seven years of the 1990s and an influential promoter of the Arch Deluxe and Campaign 55. In retrospect, the Arch Deluxe and its chicken and fish premium cousins were a timid first step into a post-Fordist approach (Cohen, 1999). Greenberg is a far bolder post-Fordist who uses the language of dynamic flexibility, decentralized management, and niche markets in his conversations about the company. "We need a different approach to management that pays more attention to market segments," he contends—contradicting the lessons allegedly learned from the Arch Deluxe (Machan, 1998). It is obvious to many McDonald's watchers on Wall Street and in the fast food sector that a synonym for Greenberg's post-Fordism is post-Krockism (Cohen, 1999).

Greenberg's attention to different market segments, niche markets, delineates a post-Fordist approach to advertising. When people had only three network choices, he argues, you could promote McDonald's with national television campaigns. Now that many people have access to 400 channels, local store-owners must be granted more freedom to spend company advertising monies in their own localities. Kroc, with his more Fordist, centralized view of management, would not have been happy with such a strategy. Unafraid to transgress the Kroc boundaries, Greenberg rewrites the Krockite bible. Where Kroc decreed that "persistence and determination *alone* are omnipotent," Greenberg confides that these are not enough. "I have to add innovation to that," he says almost nonchalantly—almost sacrilegiously (Machan, 1998). Kroc did not realize how important innovation was to the company's success, Greenberg implies, citing ideas such as enclosed dining rooms, playlands, the Big Mac, the Egg McMuffin, Ronald McDonald, Extra-Value Meals, and Happy Meals (Berman, 1998).

Where Kroc said, "Keep it simple, stupid" (Machan, 1998), Greenberg pushes innovation to the point of complexity. Literally before he was officially appointed CEO, Greenberg was already pushing the development of eight new products to the top of the corporation's priority list. Viewing his mission as *the reinvention of McDonald's*, Greenberg has promoted the Big Xtra (a whopper-like burger with lettuce and tomato), Chicken Selects (fried slices of chicken breast more reminiscent of real chicken than the "fused" McNuggets), a selection of breakfast bagel sandwiches, the McFlurry (a soft ice cream and topping concoction), the

Lobster Sandwich, the Western Breakfast Omelet, the Mexican Burger (garnished with salsa and Mexican cheese), and other innovative products. As in other post-Fordist multinationals, Greenberg plans to learn and borrow innovations from the firm's international division. Understanding the benefits of management decentralization as demonstrated by the success of the fast-growing international division, Greenberg is working to apply such strategies in U.S. operations (Machan, 1998). In this context the notion of McDonald's exerting a homogenizing effect on the world becomes even more remote. The hegemony of the twenty-first century is even more locally informed and decentralized than what occurred in the last few decades of the twentieth century.

This decentralization dynamic spills over into Greenberg's philosophy of personnel management. Pre-Greenberg management issued top-down, standardized edicts from the Oak Brook, Illinois, headquarters. Franchisees for the most part were treated in a standardized manner as delineated in the Kroc-era manual. Kroc kept it very simple in this domain, maintaining without qualification that operators and owners should do what they were told. Greenberg, in typical post-Fordist decentralized managerial style, argues that Oak Brook must listen rather than proclaim. As he attempts to change the corporation's focus and construct a new image for upper management, Greenberg has divided McDonald's into five geographic regions. Each division is headed by a divisional president and a management team who by-pass the bureaucracy and report directly to Greenberg. Combined with lay-offs of nonessential middle managers, these innovations make McDonald's more like the lean and mean post-Fordist corporations of the contemporary era (Cohen, 1999; Edwards, 1997; Machan, 1998).

The spirit of the post-Fordist corporation is, in addition to mean and lean, antiunion, downsized, and work-intensified. Greenberg wants to get fresher food to customers more quickly, increasing the pressure on already overworked, underpaid employees and making twenty-first-century labor disputes inevitable. He also wants to speed up drive-through visits, extend the installation of the new cooking systems, and equip all outlets as soon as possible with the "Made-for-you" system, which abandons the Fordist assembly-line model for a new process that facilitates employees' efforts to customize sandwiches (Berman, 1998; Pauly, 1998). Couched in the language of dynamic flexibility, the new system should force Ritzer to rethink his McDonaldization thesis (1993). If Quinlan was the "non-Kroc" of the Golden Arches, then Greenberg is the "anti-Kroc." If the new CEO's post-Fordist methods do not work quickly to turn the company's PR and marketing failures around, Big Daddy Kroc will exact his posthumous revenge with little hesitation or remorse.

Them Bad PR Blues

Like other multinational corporations, McDonald's wants its self-representations to be produced and received as seamlessly as possible in hyperreal circumstances. This is a difficult task that will become more difficult if resistance to corporate control of information grows (Vidal, 1997). The large number of anti-McDonald's protestors at rallies against George W. Bush's inauguration in January 2001 made it obvious that McDonald's had lost none of its semiotic ability to signify the abuses of transnational corporate power. Many corporations are reacting to such dissent with dirty tricks, character assassination, and legal harassment. Before

Steel and Morris made their stand, McDonald's had successfully used legal intimidation against critics including the BBC, *The Guardian* newspaper, research institutes, and countless individuals. Such bullying is more effective in Great Britain, where the burden of proof in a libel suit is on the defendant (Wilken, 1995). Now, scarred by the McLibel backlash, McDonald's executives are having to rethink their counteroperations against future detractors. The McFamily does not want to see any more headlines like the ones that ran in many world newspapers in June 1997: "McDonald's Wins Mixed Verdict in Libel Case: But International Chain Loses Publicity Battle" (Beveridge, 1997, p. 8A). Wire services framed the story this way:

> London—McDonald's won a libel case Thursday against two vegetarian activists who say they were the bigger winners in England's longest trial because they focused priceless attention on the fast-food giant's business practices.
>
> The 314-day trial left McDonald's Corp. fending off embarrassing questions after the judge said many of the sharp criticisms leveled by the activists were true.
>
> In his 800-page ruling, Justice Roger Bell said the hamburger giant was "culpably responsible" for animal cruelty and ran ad campaigns that "exploit" impressionable children. (Beveridge, 1997, p. 8A)

In McManagement's overzealous hands, the molehill became a mountain, the snowball an avalanche.

In his official ruling Judge Bell awarded McDonald's $98,000 damages for Morris and Steel's libel but affirmed the defendants' claims that the company was cruel to animals and exploited children. Attempting to "spin" the verdict as positively as possible, McDonalds executives said that they were satisfied with the ruling but confused by the judge's comments on animal cruelty. They assiduously avoided raising the issue of child exploitation—let sleeping children lie. Despite the cheers and war whoops that greeted Steel and Morris as they left the courtroom after the verdict and the praise they received (and continue to receive) around the world, executives publicly scoffed at the idea that the trial was a PR disaster (Beveridge, 1997). In this case the corporation's hegemonic control of information was leaky: Its PR staff could not overcome the appeal of the saga's David-and-Helen-versus-Goliath aspect. In a *Tom Tomorrow* cartoon strip, Sparky the penguin wondered aloud "what kind of clowns are in charge of Micky Dees?" To which an angry, cigar-puffing Ronald McDonald replied: "Watch it, penguin, or I'll have your McAss in court so fast it'll make your head spin" (quoted in Kovel, 1997, p. 27).

The Internet changes the rules for resistance to corporate power in the new century. As Joel Kovel (1997) argues, even in a trial where the parties were so unevenly matched, truths about McDonald's emerged and, thanks to the democratic features of the Internet, were "able to evade customary media censoring" (p. 26). Data about McDonald's corporate practices that might otherwise have been viewed by a few hundred people reached millions on the net's McSpotlight site. *Adbusters* ran an anti-McDonald's campaign throughout the trial that also helped establish the magazine's circulation. (Parodies of Ronald McDonald advertisements labeled "McGrease" or "McShit" still appear in *Adbusters*; see Groves, 1996). Such representations exert a powerful subversive effect on carefully inscribed McDonald's signifiers: I have spotted numerous Ronald McDonald McShit and McGrease posters on the walls of adolescents' rooms and imagined the look of horror they would inspire in McDonald's PR department. Yikes, they might exclaim, what happened to those little kids who used to crawl around our McPlayground? In hyperreality, the signifier, though powerful, is notoriously fickle.

In order to interrupt the damaging practices of multinational corporations, critics must be able to convince increasing numbers of people of the complexity of power and its capacity to ingratiate itself into individual hearts and minds and larger cultural, political, and economic structures. This hegemonic, ideological, semiotic, and pedagogical dynamic may be complex, but people can be understand it when it is explained to them in an accessible manner.

In my experience, whenever I try to explain power, people are able to extend my notion and my explanatory ability by offering rich examples and metaphors from their own encounters with it. A burger is never simply a burger, and the cultural domain is now also the primary political domain. Until we learn these lessons, corporate power-wielders in the twenty-first century will continue to change our world and our minds in undesirable ways. To prevent such unhealthy mutations, we must learn to read the sign of the burger in a culture of power—not simply as an end in itself, but as an avenue to understanding more clearly what we have become. In this less refracted context we may be better prepared to discard the semiotically expended "American Dream" and create a more complex and just global dream—a global dream where American optimism plays a socially responsible role.

References

Advertising Age. 1991. "McDonald's Takes Leap Into Trouble." *Advertising Age* 62:41 (September 30), p. 41.

Affleck, J. 1998. "Teenage McDonald's Workers Go on Strike." *News and Observer* (Raleigh, N.C.), April 17.

Airakinsen, T. 1992. "The Rhetoric of Domination." In T. E. Wartenberg, ed., *Rethinking Power.* Albany: State University of New York Press.

Alfino, M. 1998. "Postmodern Hamburgers: Taking a Postmodern Attitude Toward McDonald's." In M. Alfino, J. Caputo, and R. Wynyard, eds., *McDonaldization Revisited: Critical Essays on Consumer Culture.* Westport, Conn.: Praeger.

Amad, P. 1996. *Virtual Cultures* 4. Available from: <http://www.mcs.mq. edu.au/content/VirtualCultures/vc7-amad-paper>.

American Libraries. 1993. "ALA/McDonald's Team Up Again for Reading Program." *American Libraries* 24:11, p. 1047.

Anthony, T. 1997. "McDonald's Moves Into All Segments of Society." *Centre Daily Times* (State College, Pa.), July 15, p. 3A.

Antique Appeal. 1996. "Ronald McDonald Head for Sale." Available from: <http://www.antiqueappeal.com>.

Apple, M. 1996. "Dominance and Dependency: Situating *The Bell Curve* Within the Conservative Restoration." In J. L. Kincheloe, S. R. Steinberg, and A. D. Gresson, eds., *Measured Lies: The Bell Curve Examined.* New York: St. Martin's Press.

Arch Deluxe Hate Mail. 1997. Available from: <http://omni.cc.purdue. edu/~royald/letters.htm>.

Aronowitz, S. 1983. "The Relativity of Theory." *Village Voice*, no. 27 (December), p. 60.

Aronowitz, S., and W. DiFazio. 1994. *The Jobless Future: Sci-tech and the Dogma of Work.* Minneapolis: University of Minnesota Press.

Aronowitz, S., and H. Giroux. 1991. *Postmodern Education: Politics, Culture, and Social Criticism.* Minneapolis: University of Minnesota Press.

Associated Press. 1998. "Business Briefly." *Morning News Tribune* (Tacoma, Wash.), June 2.

Bak, S. 1997. "McDonald's in Seoul: Food Choices, Identity, and Nationalism." In J. Watson, ed., *Golden Arches East: McDonald's in East Asia.* Stanford: Stanford University Press.

Bastable, J. 1993. "From Russia with Special Sauce." *Mademoiselle* 99:12, pp. 98, 106.

Bell, D., and G. Valentine. 1997. *Consuming Geography: We Are What We Eat.* New York: Routledge.

Benezra, K. 1995. "To Live and Tie-in LA." *Brandweek* 36:31 (August 7), pp. 23–24.

Berman, S. 1998. "Cheeseburger Baron Hails from Chicago Tribe." *Forward* 102 (August 28), p. 31.

Bessman, J. 1989. "McDonald's Vid Deal Judged a McPlus for Sell-thru." *Billboard* 101:40 (October 7), p. 93.

Best, S., and D. Kellner. 1991. *Postmodern Theory: Critical Interrogations.* New York: Guilford Press.

Beveridge, D. 1997. "McDonald's Wins Libel Case." *Centre Daily Times,* June 20, p. 8A.

Bizzell, P. 1991. "Power, Authority, and Critical Pedagogy." *Journal of Basic Writing* 10:2, pp. 54–70.

Black Enterprise. 1988. "Robert Beavers: The Apostle of the Golden Arches." *Black Enterprise* 18:7, p. 86.

Block, F. 1990. *Postindustrial Possibilities: A Critique of Economic Discourse.* Berkeley: University of California Press.

Boas, A. M., and S. Chain. 1976. *Big Mac: The Unauthorized Story of McDonald's.* New York: E. P. Dutton.

Boyles, D. 1998. *American Education and Corporations: The Free Market Goes to School.* New York: Garland.

Bremmer, B., and G. DeGeorge. 1989. "The Burger Wars Were Just a Warmup for McDonald's." *Business Week,* May 8, pp. 67, 70.

"Burger Queen." 1999. "This Debate Seems To Be Stuck in a Loop." Available from: <http://www.mcspotlight.org/debate/meds/messages/4101.html>.

Calinescu, M. 1987. *Five Faces of Modernity: Modernism, Avant-garde, Decadence, Kitsch, Modernism.* Durham, N.C.: Duke University Press.

Caputo, J. 1998. "The Rhetoric of McDonaldization: A Social Semiotic Perspective." In M. Alfino, J. S. Caputo, and R. Wynyard, eds., *McDonaldization Revisited: Critical Essays on Consumer Culture.* Westport, Conn.: Praeger.

Charlie X. 1994. "Screwing Over Your Local McDonald's." *Phrack Magazine* 5:45 (March 30), unpaginated [pp. 1–6].

Cohen, D. 1999. "New McDonald's CEO Improves Its Image." *Chicago Sun-Times,* January 31.

Collins, A. 1994. "Intellectuals, Power, and Quality Television." In H. Giroux and P. McLaren, eds., *Between Borders: Pedagogy and the Politics of Cultural Studies*. New York: Routledge.

Collins, S. 1998. Review of James Watson, ed., *Golden Arches East: McDonald's in East Asia*. Available from: <http//www.mcs.net/~zupko/cs_book.htm>.

Consumer Reports. 1988. "A Survival Guide to the Greasy Kid Stuff." *Consumer Reports* 53:6, pp. 355–61.

Cooper, D. 1994. "Productive, Relational, and Everywhere? Conceptualising Power and Resistance Within Foucauldian Feminism." *Sociology* 28, pp. 435–454.

Cooper, M. 1998. "General Pinochet Still Rules: Twenty-five Years After Allende—An Anti-Memoir." *The Nation* 266:10 (March 23), pp. 11, 23.

CQ Researcher. 1991. "Fast Food's Most Visible Target." *CQ Researcher* 1:25 (November 8), p. 831.

Crescenzo, S. 1997. "Trouble Under the Golden Arches: The American Icon's PR Crisis." Available from: <http://prsa.org/sept97mc.html>.

Critical Art Ensemble. 1994. *The Electronic Disturbance*. Brooklyn, N.Y.: Autonomedia.

Deetz, S. 1993. "Corporations, the Media Industry, and Society: Ethical Imperatives and Responsibilities." Paper presented to the International Communication Association, Washington, D.C.

Deveny, K. 1988. "Meet Mike Quinlan, Big Mac's Attack CEO." *Business Week*, no. 3051 (May 9), pp. 92, 94, 97.

Dewey, J. 1916. *Democracy and Education*. New York: Free Press.

du Gay, P., S. Hall, L. Janes, H. MacKay, and K. Negus. 1997. *Doing Cultural Studies: The Story of the Sony Walkman*. London: Sage Publications.

Economist, The. 1996. "MacWorld." *The Economist*, June 29, pp. 61–62.

Edwards, C. 1997. "Ed Rens: Retires as McDonald's Domestic President; Regional Heads Named." Available from: <http://www.sddt.com/files.librarywire/97wireheadlines.07-97>.

———. 1999. "McDonald's Names U.S. Marketing Chief." AP Online. January 19.

Ellis, J. 1986. Review of John Love, *McDonald's: Behind the Arches*. *Business Week*, no. 2968 (October 13), pp. 18–22.

Emery, T. 1997. "Group Hits Disney, McDonald's Over Toy Factory Conditions." *Boston Globe*, May 3. Available from: <http://www.nlcnet.org/press/newsclip/globe.htm>.

"Expelled French Activist Bové Gets Standing Ovation at Anti-Globalization Forum." 2001. January 30. Available from: <http://njpcgreens.org/brasil.html>.

Featherstone, Liza. 1998. "The Burger International." *Left Business Observer* 86. Available from: <http://www.panix.com/~dhenwood/McDonalds. html>.

―――. 1999. "The Burger International Revisited." *Left Business Observer* 91. Available from: <http://www.panix.com/~dhenwood/ McDonalds2.html>.

Feder, B. 1997. "Where Have You Gone, Ray Kroc?" *New York Times*, June 5.

Fischer, P., et al. 1991. "Brand Logo Recognition by Children Aged 3 to 6 Years." *Journal of the American Medical Association* 266:22, pp. 3145–48.

Fiske, J. 1993. *Power Plays, Power Works*. New York: Verso.

Flynn, G. 1996. "McDonald's Serves Up HR Excellence." *Personnel Journal* 75:1, pp. 54–55.

Garfield, B. 1992. "Nice Ads, McDonald's, but That Theme Not What You Want." *Advertising Age* 63:8 (February 24), p. 53.

Gergen, K. 1991. *The Saturated Self: Dilemmas of Identity in Everyday Life*. New York: Basic Books.

Giroux, H. 1994. *Disturbing Pleasures: Learning Popular Culture*. New York: Routledge.

Giroux, H. 1996. "Slacking Off: Border Youth and Postmodern Education." In H. Giroux, C. Lankshear, P. McLaren, and M. Peters, eds., *Counternarratives: Cultural Studies and Critical Pedagogies in Postmodern Space*. New York: Routledge.

Goldman, R. 1992. *Reading Ads Socially*. New York: Routledge.

Goldman, R., and S. Papson. 1994. "The Postmodernism That Failed." In D. Dickens and A. Fontana, eds., *Postmodernism and Social Inquiry*. New York: Guilford Press.

―――. 1996. *Sign Wars: The Cluttered Landscape of Advertising*. New York: Guilford Press.

Gottdiener, M. 1995. *Postmodern Semiotics: Material Culture and the Forms of Postmodern Life*. Cambridge, Mass.: Blackwell.

Green, R. 2001. "Forced Apology Sparks Debate." *Hartford Courant*, June 3. Available from: <http://www.raptorial.com/HOF/Kading01.html>.

"Gromit." 1999. "McDonald's Rocks―I Should Know." March 26. Available from: <http://www.mcspotlight.org/debate/meds/messages/405z.html>.

Grossberg, L. 1992. *We Gotta Get Out of This Place*. New York: Routledge.

Groves, J. 1996. "McDonald's Morale Crumbling." *Adbusters*. Winter.

Hamilton, M. 1997. "Taking Its McLumps." *Washington Post*, August 17, pp. H1, H6.

Hancock, P. 1997. Review of George Ritzer, *The McDonaldization of Society*, rev. ed. Available from: <http://www.mngt.waikato.ac.nz/depts/sml/ journal/indexv11/Hancock.htm>.

Harvey, D. 1989. *The Conditions of Postmodernity*. Cambridge, Mass.: Basil Blackwell.

Hinchey, P. 1998. *Finding Freedom in the Classroom: A Practical Introduction to Critical Theory*. New York: Peter Lang.

Hoffman, H. 2001. "Want Fries with That Humiliation?" *New Haven Advocate*, June 14. Available from: <http://www.raptorial.com/HOF/Kading04.html>.

Horovitz, B. 1998a. "My Job Is Always on the Line." *USA Today*, March 16, p. 8B.

———. 1998b. "McDonald's Gives Beanies Another Try." *USA Today*, May 18, p. 4B.

Hume, S. 1993. "Fast-food Caught in the Middle." *Advertising Age* 64:6, pp. 12–15.

Hundley, T. 1997. "It's Been a Proven Fact: Peace Follows Franchise." *Centre Daily Times* (State College, Pa.), July 15, p. 3A.

Jatkinson, B. 1998. "My Beef with McDonald's." *Virginian Pilot and Ledger Star* (Norfolk, Va.), June 11.

"Jay W." 1999. "Why Do I Look Down Upon This Great Company." April 7. Available from: <http://www.mcspotlight.org/debate/mcds/messages/4110.html>.

Jeffress, L. (with J. Mayanobe). 2001. "A World Struggle Is Underway: An Interview with José Bové." *Z Magazine* (June). Available from: <http://www.thirdworldtraveler.com/Reforming_System/World_Struggle_Underway.html>.

"Jen." 1999. "McDonald's Irritating Customers." March 29. Available from: <http://www.mcspotlight.org/debate/meds/messages/4068.html>.

"R Jenkins." 1999. "Exploiting." March 23. Available from: <http://www.mcspotlight.org/debate/mcds/messages/4018.html>.

Katayama, F. 1986. "Japan's Big Mac." *Fortune* 114:6 (September 15), pp. 114–20.

"Kati." 1999. "Annoying Customers and Why I'm Annoyed with Stupidity." March 30. Available from: <http://www.mcspotlight.org/debate/mcds/messages/4076.html>.

Kaye, L. 1992. "Traveller's Tales." *Far Eastern Economic Review* (June 11), p. 26.

Keat, R. 1994. "Skepticism, Authority, and the Market." In R. Keat, N. Whiteley, and N. Abercrombie, eds., *The Authority of the Consumer*. New York: Routledge.

Kellner, D. 1989. *Critical Theory, Marxism, and Modernity*. Baltimore: Johns Hopkins University Press.

———. 1990. *Television and the Crisis of Democracy*. Boulder, Colo.: Westview.

———. 1992. "Popular Culture and the Construction of Postmodern Identities." In S. Lash and J. Friedman, eds., *Modernity and Identity*. Cambridge, Mass.: Blackwell.

———. 1998. "Foreword: McDonaldization and Its Discontents." In M. Alfino, J. Caputo, and R. Wynyard, eds., *McDonaldization Revisited: Critical Essays on Consumer Culture*. Westport, Conn.: Praeger.

Khalili, I. 2001. "Israeli Police Arrest French Farmer in West Bank." June 21. Available from: <http://www.shianews.com/hi/middle_east/news_id/0000506.php>.

Kincheloe, J. 1995. *Toil and Trouble: Good Work, Smart Workers, and the Integration of Academic and Vocational Education*. New York: Peter Lang.

———. 1999. *How Do We Tell the Workers: The Socio-economic Foundations of Work and Vocational Education*. Boulder, Colo.: Westview.

Kincheloe, J., and S. Steinberg 1997. *Changing Multiculturalism: New Times, New Curriculum*. London: Open University Press.

Kirk, J. 1997. "McDonald's 'Campaign 55' Can't Seem to Get a Break." *Centre Daily Times*, June 17, p. 5B.

Kovel, J. 1997. "Bad News for Fast Food: What's Wrong with McDonald's?" *Z Magazine*, September, pp. 26–31.

Kramer, L. 1997. "Jack Greenberg." *Nation's Restaurant News* 31:4 (January), p. 76.

Kroc, R. 1977. *Grinding It Out: The Making of McDonald's*. New York: St. Martin's Paperbacks.

Lash, S. 1990. *Sociology of Postmodernism*. New York: Routledge.

Lawren, B. 1993. "McRobot." *Omni* 15:7 (May), p. 29.

Leidner, R. 1993. *Fast Food, Fast Talk: Service Work and the Routinization of Everyday Life*. Berkeley: University of California Press.

Love, J. 1986. *McDonald's: Behind the Arches*. New York: Bantam Books.

———. 1995. *McDonald's: Behind the Arches*. 2d ed. New York: Bantam Books.

"Luke Kuhn." 1999. "Big Mac with a Side Order of Pepper Spray?" March 3. Available from: <http://www.mcspotlight.org/debate/mcds/messages/3929.html>.

Luke, T. 1991. "Touring Hyperreality: Critical Theory Confronts Informational Society." In P. Wexler, *Critical Theory Now*. New York: Falmer Press.

Luxenberg, S. 1985. *Roadside Empires: How the Chains Franchised*. New York: Viking Penguin.

McCarthy, T. 1992. "The Critique of Impure Reason: Foucault and the Frankfurt School." In T. Wartenberg, ed., *Rethinking Power*. Albany, N.Y.: SUNY Press.

McCormick, M. 1993. "Kid Rhino and McDonald's Enter Licensing Agreement." *Billboard* 105:8 (February 2), pp. 10, 81.

McDonald's Customer Relations Center. 1994. Handout to schools.

McDonald's Handout from Adelaide Zoo. 1999. "Improving Our Environment." November. Adelaide, Australia.

"McDonald's Replaces Its Chief Executive." 1998. *Star-Tribune* (Minneapolis–St. Paul), May 1.

Macedo, D. 1994. *Literacies of Power: What Americans Are Not Allowed To Know.* Boulder, Colo.: Westview.

Machan, D. 1988. "Great Hash Browns, but Watch Those Biscuits." *Forbes* 142:6 (September 19), pp. 192–96.

———. 1998. "Polishing the Golden Arches." *Forbes Global,* June 15, pp. 1–3.

McLaren, P. 1991. "Schooling and the Postmodern Body: Critical Pedagogy and the Politics of Enfleshment." In H. Giroux, ed., *Postmodernism, Feminism, and Cultural Politics: Redrawing Educational Boundaries.* Albany, N.Y.: SUNY Press.

———. 1994. "Multiculturalism and the Postmodern Critique: Toward a Pedagogy of Resistance and Transformation." In H. Giroux and P. McLaren, *Between Borders: Pedagogy and the Politics of Cultural Studies.* New York: Routledge.

———. 1997. Revolutionary Multiculturalism: Pedagogies of Dissent for the New Millennium. Boulder, Colo.: Westview Press.

McLaren, P., R. Hammer, S. Reilly, and D. Sholle. 1995. *Rethinking Media Literacy: A Critical Pedagogy of Representation.* New York: Peter Lang.

MacLean's. 1994. "Rejecting McUnion." *MacLean's* 107:10 (March 7), p. 43.

McLibel Newsletter. 1997. Available from: <http://www.mcspotlight.org>.

McSpotlight. 1997–. Available from: <http://www.mcspotlight.org>.

Manning, P., and B. Cullum-Swan. 1994. "Narrative, Content, and Semiotic Analysis." In N. Denzin and Y. Lincoln, eds., *Handbook of Qualitative Research.* Thousands Oaks, Calif.: Sage.

Marks, K. 1998. "Big Mac at 30 No Longer the Burger King." *The Independent* (London), September 5.

Martin, H., and H. Schumann. 1997. *The Global Trap: Globalization and the Assault on Democracy and Prosperity.* New York: Zed Books.

"Mike Bacon." 1999. "Ah! Sour Grapes! Would You Like an Enema with That?" Available from: <http://www.mcspotlight.org/debate/mcds/messages/4078.html>.

Miles, S. 1998. "McDonaldization and the Global Sports Store: Constructing Consumer Meanings in a Rationalized Society." In M. Alfino, J. Caputo, and R. Wynyard, eds., *McDonaldization Revisited: Critical Essays on Consumer Culture.* Westport, Conn.: Praeger.

Mintz, S. 1997. "Afterword: Swallowing Modernity." In J. Watson, ed., *Golden Arches East: McDonald's in East Asia.* Stanford: Stanford University Press.

Monniger, J. 1988. "Fast Food." *American Heritage* 39:3 (April), pp. 68–75.

Morris, C. 1994. "McDonald's: Not Retailers' Kind of Place." *Billboard* 106:30 (July 23), pp. 3, 127.

Moser, P. 1988. "The McDonald's Mystique." *Fortune*, July 4, pp. 112–16.

Mumby, D. 1989. "Ideology and the Social Construction of Meaning: A Communication Perspective." *Communication Quarterly* 37:4, pp. 291–304.

Musolf, R. 1992. "Structure, Institutions, Power, and Ideology: New Directions Within Symbolic Interactionism." *Sociological Quarterly* 33:2, pp. 171–89.

Newman, M. 1994. "McDonald's/EMI Sales Break 9 million." *Billboard* 106:42 (October 15), pp. 6, 199.

Newman, P. 1988. "Cohon's Hamburger Diplomacy." *MacLean's* 101:23 (May 30), p. 44.

Neilson, J. 1999. *Warring Fictions: American Literary Culture and the Vietnam War Narrative.* Oxford, Miss.: University of Mississippi Press.

Neuborne, E. 1999. "Generation Y." *Business Week* 36:16 (February 15), pp. 80–88.

Noble, B. 2000. "French Fried Over Micky Dees." Available from: <http://www.topicsmag.com/1200/feature2.htm>.

Official Happy Meals Web Site. 1999–. Available from: <http://www.mcdonalds.com/countries/usa/whatsnew/happy_meal>.

Ola, P., and E. D'Aulaire. 1988. "60 Billion Burgers and Counting." *Reader's Digest* 131:788, pp. 39–45.

Parker, M. 1998. "Nostalgia and Mass Culture: McDonaldization and Cultural Elitism." In M. Alfino, J. Caputo, and R. Wynyard, eds., *McDonaldization Revisited: Critical Essays on Consumer Culture.* Westport, Conn.: Praeger.

Pauly, H. 1998. "McDonald's Predicts Growth." *Chicago Sun-Times*, May 22.

Peace, A. 1990. "Dropping Out of Sight: Social Anthropology Encounters Postmodernism." *Australian Journal of Anthropology* 1:1, pp. 18–31.

People. 1988. "McDharma's." *People Magazine* 29:17 (May 2), p. 81.

Personnel Journal. 1994. "Global Companies Reexamine Corporate Culture." *Personnel Journal*, August, pp. 12–13.

"Philip." 1996. "The McDonald's of the Damned." Available from: <http://etext.archive.Umich.edu/zines/friends/phil/archive/96/mcdamned-htm>.

Raptorial Hall of Fame. 2001. Available from: <http://www.raptorial.com/HOF/Kading.html>.

Rikert, D. 1980. "McDonald's Corporation." Harvard Business School Case Study. Boston.

Ritzer, G. 1993. *The McDonaldization of Society.* Thousand Oaks, Calif.: Pine Forge Press.

———. 1998. "Slow Food Versus McDonald's." *International Herald of Tastes* 10, July–September.

Rorty, A. 1992. "Power and Powers: A Dialogue Between Buff and Rebuff." In T. Wartenberg, ed., *Rethinking Power.* Albany, N.Y.: SUNY Press.

Salva-Ramirez, M. 1995–96. "McDonald's: A Prime Example of a Corporate Culture." *Public Relations Quarterly* 40:4, pp. 30–32.

Schiller, H. 1993. "Transnational Media: Creating Consumers Worldwide." *Journal of International Affairs* 47, pp. 47–58.

Schlosser, E. 1998a. "Fast-food Nation, Part One: The True Cost of America's Diet." *Rolling Stone,* September 3.

———. 1998b. "Meat and Potatoes." *Rolling Stone,* November 26.

———. 2001. *Fast Food Nation: The Dark Side of the All-American Meal.* Boston: Houghton Mifflin.

Seidman, G. 1999. "Protesters Steal Limelight at WTO." November 29. Available from: <http://www.msnbc.com/news/340513.asp>.

Seiter, E. 1993. *Sold Separately: Parents and Children in Consumer Culture.* New Brunswick, N.J.: Rutgers University Press.

"Sharon." 1999. "The Customers Aren't Going to Change." March 31. Available from: <http://www.mcspotlight.org/debate/mcds/messages/4084.html>.

"Shaun." 1999. "Most Customers Are Not Annoying, It May Be You." April 1. Available from: <http://www.mcspotlight.org/debate/mcds/messages/4088.html>.

Shelton, A. 1995. "Where the Big Mac Is King: McDonald's U.S.A." *Taboo: The Journal of Culture and Education* 1:2, pp. 1–15.

Shiva, V. 1997. "Vandana Shiva on McDonald's Exploitation and the Global Economy." Available from: <http://www.mcspotlight.org/people/interviews/vandanatranscripts.html>.

Smart, B. 1992. *Modern Conditions, Postmodern Controversies.* New York: Routledge.

Solomon, A., and S. Hume. 1991. "Hot Fast-food Ideas Cool Off." *Advertising Age* 62:41 (September 30), p. 42.

Solomon, C. 1996. "Big Mac's McGlobal HR secrets." *Personnel Journal* 75:4, pp. 46–54.

Stein, S. 1997. "Witness Statement." October 24. Available from: <http://www.mcspotlight.org/people/witness/employment/stein.html>.

Steinberg, S., and J. Kincheloe, eds. 1997. *Kinderculture: The Corporate Construction of Childhood.* Boulder, Colo.: Westview.

"Store Manager." 1999. "Why Do I Work for This Great Company?" April 1. Available from: <http://www.mcspotlight.org/debate/mcds/messages/4089.html>.

Tefft, S. 1994. "China Imposes Brakes on Influx of Foreign Funds." *Christian Science Monitor*, December 21, p. 41.

"Think Global, Think Protest." 2000. January 7. Available from: <http://www.smh.com.au/news/0007/01/text/review6.html>.

Thompson, J. 1987. "Language and Ideology: A Framework for Analysis." *Sociological Review* 35, pp. 516–36.

"Tony Tiger." 1999. "Great Company Says Who?" April 5. Available from: <http://www.mcspotlight.org/debate/mcds/messages/4102.html>.

Toy Zone. 1999. "Unofficial McDonald's Happy Meal information." Available from: <http://www.thetoyzone.com/mcfaq.html>.

US McLibel Support Campaign Newsletter. 1997.

Vidal, J. 1997. *McLibel: Burger Culture on Trial*. London: Macmillan.

Wa Mwachofi, N. 1998. "Missing the Cultural Bias of Irrationality in the McDonaldization of Society." In M. Alfino, J. Caputo, and R. Wynyard, eds., *McDonaldization Revisited: Critical Essays on Consumer Culture*. Westport, Conn.: Praeger.

Wartenberg, T. 1992. "Introduction." In T. Wartenberg, ed., *Rethinking Power*. Albany, N.Y.: SUNY Press.

Wasserstrom, J. 1998. "Burgers, Bowling, and the Myth of Americanizing China." *Dissent*, Fall, pp. 22–25.

Watson, J. 1997a. "Preface." In J. Watson, ed., *Golden Arches East: McDonald's in East Asia*. Stanford: Stanford University Press.

———. 1997b. "Introduction: Transnationalism, Localization, and Fast Foods in East Asia." In J. Watson, ed., *Golden Arches East: McDonald's in East Asia*. Stanford: Stanford University Press.

———. 1997c. "McDonald's in Hong Kong: Consumerism, Dietary Change, and the Rise of a Children's Culture." In J. Watson, ed., *Golden Arches East: McDonald's in East Asia*. Stanford: Stanford University Press.

Weinstein, J. 1993. "Falling Arches." *Village Voice* 38:26, June 29, p. 42.

Whalen, J. 1994a. "McDonald's Cafe Dishes Up Service." *Advertising Age* 65:1, January 3, p. 36.

———. 1994b. "McDonald's To Go Homey in That Unit." *Advertising Age* 65:23, May 30, p. 2.

Wheeler, T. 2001. "José Bové of Millau—A Farmer for Our Time." April 6. Available from: <http://www.counterpunch.org/bove.html>.

Whitney-Smith, E. 2001. "Cain and Abel: Scarcity, Information, and the Invention of War." Available from: <http://www.well.com/user/elin/cain.htm>.

Wilken, E. 1995. "Big Mac Attack." *World Watch* 8:4, July, pp. 6–7.

Williams, F. 2001. "José Bové: The New Leader of the Global Food Revolt." *Outside* Magazine (June). Available from: <http://www.purefood.org/gefood/SaviorBove.cfm>.

Wood, C., and A. Wilson-Smith. 1988. "A Bolshoi-Mak Attack." *MacLean's* 101:21, May 16, p. 30.

Wood, R. 1998. "Old Wine in New Bottles: Critical Limitations of the McDonaldization Thesis—The Case of Hospitality Services." In M. Alfino, J. Caputo, and R. Wynyard, eds., *McDonaldization Revisited: Critical Essays on Consumer Culture*. Westport, Conn.: Praeger.

Wu, D. 1997. "McDonald's in Taipei: Hamburgers, Betel Nuts, and National Identity." In J. Watson, ed., *Golden Arches East: McDonald's in East Asia*. Stanford: Stanford University Press.

Wynyard, R. 1998. "The Bunless Burger." In M. Alfino, J. Caputo, and R. Wynyard, eds., *McDonaldization Revisited: Critical Essays on Consumer Culture*. Westport, Conn.: Praeger.

Yakabuski, K. 1997. "Teamsters Taking Another Run at a McDonald's Outlet." *Globe and Mail* (Toronto), March 6.

Yan, Y. 1997. "McDonald's in Beijing: The Localization of Americana." In J. Watson, ed., *Golden Arches East: McDonald's in East Asia*. Stanford: Stanford University Press.

Zayani, M. 1997. "Review of George Ritzer, *McDonaldization of Society*, 2nd Edition." *Criticism* 39:4, pp. 1–4.

Index

227

Müller